The Quanders—Since 1684,

AN ENDURING AFRICAN AMERICAN LEGACY

The Quander Family's History and Legacy is more than an African American story. Rather, it is a full component of American history. Read, savor, learn, enjoy, and share the knowledge of how those of us who are descendant sons and daughters of Africa mightily contributed to, and sustained in the creation of the nation.

ROHULAMIN QUANDER, author

ROHULAMIN QUANDER

ISBN 978-1-0980-7093-9 (paperback)
ISBN 978-1-0980-7695-5 (hardcover)
ISBN 978-1-0980-7094-6 (digital)

Christian Faith Publishing, Inc.
832 Park Avenue
Meadville, PA 16335
www.christianfaithpublishing.com

Printed in the United States of America

CONTENTS

Omnipotence of God

IN PRAISE OF *THE QUANDER STORY*

·✦✦✦✦·

Few families, other than Native Americans, can show detailed evidence of an American heritage that spans well over three centuries. Even fewer can identify foreparents whose lives intersect with George Washington, the first president of the United States, and Francis Scott Key, the lawyer who penned the inspiring verses of the National Anthem. In Rohulamin Quander's remarkable narrative—made even more remarkable by being an African American story—such historical evidence appears as early as the 1670s in the Catholic-founded colony of Maryland. Acquiring freedom from slavery by their master's will in 1684, Henry and Margrett Quando began the record of the Quander family's long journey and its repetition of names, sustained religious faith, and commitment to equal justice and personal achievement throughout the many generations. The book's exhaustive documentation and compilation of court cases, state archives, probate records such as the will of George Washington, census data, street names, newspaper articles, and historic sites bring to life the Quander men and women and their experiences in Maryland, Virginia, and Washington, D.C. from the seventeenth to the twenty-first century. *The Quander Story* thus represents many stories of kinship that chronicle the ties that bind and sometimes fray, but ultimately unite in a shared memory, recurrent family reunions, and the eventual discovery of the family's African ancestral roots in the Amaquandoh family of Accra, Ghana.

Evelyn Brooks Higginbotham
Victor S. Thomas Professor of History and of
African and African American Studies,
Harvard University
National President, The Association for the Study
of African American Life and History

ACKNOWLEDGMENTS

My dear wife, Carmen, who always believes in and encourages me to go forward and aim higher. She is my shining star.

To my adult children—Iliana, Rohulamin II, and Fatima—they always make me look good in all that I do.

To James W. Quander and Joheora Rohualamin Quander, my loving parents, always dedicated and focused upon instilling Christian values and a moral standing into me and my siblings.

All Amkwandoh (Amaquandoh) ancestors in Ghana, who—in their suffering and sustained indignity—created the foundation upon which this story, an American history story, is built.

All my Quando/Quander ancestors, who were involuntarily brought to this land then enslaved only in body but never in their minds. I give you my highest praise.

All my Quander ancestors, whether born free or enslaved as of January 1, 1863, I thank you. Your presence and contributors made this history. Without you, there would be no story to share and tell.

Gladys Quander Tancil, storyteller, sustainer, overlay of this product, always with some new information, and likewise encouraging me to move forward and share *The Quander Story*.

And Elaine Eldridge, my editor, my wordsmith, she guided me in telling the story without losing any of the essence of the history. She really helped me to make it happen.

The Quander Story and all that it represents in memoriam to George Floyd (May 25, 2020) a soul brother who died too soon at the hands of the sustained racism and indignities that, since 1619, continue to daily characterize African American lives. Indeed, *we can't breathe!* George never intended to be a hero nor did he ever plan to be a martyr. But his life and the manner and circumstances of his untimely death underscore to all of us how fleetingly insignificant a Black life in the United States can be. In dying—a lynching if you will—he unleashed the hurt, both physically and psychologically, that has been pent up in the African American community for 401 years. The outpouring of recent events, generously embraced by our Caucasian brothers and sisters, have indeed underscored that *Black lives do matter.*

The Quander Story to John Edward (1883–1950) and Maude Pearson Quander (1880–1962), my loving grandparents. Their love of family and determination to save my father James W. Quander's life, as a child diabetic, is without equal. Through them and my dad, *The Quander Story* lives and has been preserved. Thank you.

INTRODUCTION

As you turn these pages, place yourself into the atmosphere in which the African American—focused stories or occasions unfold. See yourself in the struggle facing and overcoming obstacles, many of which were racially motivated. As you progress from decade to decade and century to century, also grasp the sense of place, the disappointments, but still the triumphs of the people whose stories are told here. The refusal to be beaten! Only then can you fully appreciate how some of the ancestors' achievements, while seeming insignificant by application of twenty-first-century standards, were milestones at the time. From personal enslavement to freedom in a single life or perhaps only one generation beyond, there was an unquenchable thirst to achieve. Whether by formal education, operating a business, or acquiring land to farm, these men and women were determined to do better, to do more, and to prove themselves to themselves.

What you are about to read, *The Quander Story*, is but one example of American history. Whether it be African American, European American, or otherwise, it is—more than anything else— an American story. Regretfully, our nation continues to experience racial attitudes and divisions that drive us apart and reject our shared stories. The murder of George Floyd in Minneapolis on May 25, 2020, unsheathed a two-edged sword. One sharp edge—"I can't breathe!"—underscores the continuing frustration, suffering, hurt, and anger African Americans have sustained since 1619, when the first enslaved and chained ancestors were involuntarily transported from Africa to Virginia. Yet the other sharp edge has cut an opening through which much long-standing apathy has been exposed, cutting away the lack of awareness, concern, and understanding of what African Americans (the other side) have endured for centuries.

America is changing as people of all races and especially a large contingent of American Whites have stepped forward, joined arms with their black, brown, and yellow brothers and sisters, and cried, "Enough already!"

Is this the beginning of a new America? I certainly hope so. And the new America cannot come a moment too soon! African Americans built this country despite the initial denial of the appellation "American" as a component of our identity. Our uncompensated labor from sunrise to sunset built the U.S. Capitol, the White House, George Washington's Mount Vernon, other presidential plantation estate mansions, and the Smithsonian Castle and even initiated the pre-Civil War construction of the Washington Monument. The enslaved constructed the streets in Washington, DC, upon which the enslavers rode in their well-appointed carriages to sites where they enjoyed the various attractions and accumulated riches. What thought was given to the enslaved Africans who labored to create these comforts? Little to none! This book, although it cannot tell all their stories or make up for that lack of thought, is my contribution to telling the story of American history.

On August 11, 1968, I attended my first Quander family reunion. The times were turbulent. Dr. Martin Luther King Jr. and Senator Robert F. Kennedy had been assassinated earlier that year, and the nation was still in a great uproar. Prior to the reunion, as I prepared to enter my last year as a student at the Howard University School of Law and assume the presidency of the student bar association, I had little thought of where I had come from or what "To Be a Quander" meant.[1] But the reunion piqued my interest in my history and reminded me that for years, as I served as an international pal, interacting with foreign students, I was routinely called "Mr. Quando" by some of the students from West African nations. Initially, it meant nothing, perhaps just a mispronunciation of my surname. But the seeming error occurred too often. It made me think. One day, I asked one of the students, who happened to be a Ghanaian, "What's this about? Why do all these students call me 'Mr. Quando?'"

"You mean you don't know?" he asked in return. "Your name is Fanti, one of our Ghanaian ethnic groups. In Ghana, the name is 'Amkwandoh,' and anywhere you go in Ghana and tell someone 'I am Quando,' they will immediately hear 'Amkwandoh' and recognize it for what it is—a Fanti name."

Curious about his insistence about our surname, I asked older family members if they had ever heard the name "Quando." One very senior cousin said he heard from even older relatives that our name used to be spelled differently. "Back there somewhere," he told me, pointing over his shoulder, "they said the U.S. census taker made a spelling error and dropped the *o* and added *er*." But no one knew exactly when "back there somewhere" was. Researching seventeenth- and eighteenth-century records verified the Quando name and showed that the "back there somewhere" error did indeed occur in the U.S. Census of 1800. My later research reflects that both spellings, *Quando* and *Quander*, existed into the nineteenth century, finally resting with the "er" spelling.

Armed with this tidbit of information, you are ready to begin what is now widely appreciated as *The Quander Story*. Reading this book, you are embarking upon a more than 350-year journey, a legacy that stretches from the depths of abduction and enslavement to the heights of national acclaim. What did it mean to be an American who was enslaved by George Washington? How do their descendants feel about that situation? How are the Quanders different but likewise similar to other African American families? Inherent in this history are the lows of racial discrimination and mistreatment and the many and continuing successes that Quanders have enjoyed through the centuries. Perhaps this poem by Lewis Lear Quander captures from whence we came.

Miracle of Faith
(Tribute to My Mount Vernon Ancestors)

Imagine sir if you could be
Back in 1793,
Remembering the things that you crave
But cannot hope for—you're a slave.
Freedom was a dirty word;
Only something that you'd heard.
It certainly don't apply to you
And there's nothing you can do.
Just pick that cotton, hoe that corn,
Wish that you were never born.
Your culture has been lost for years
And there you stand reduced to tears.

To be so helpless, yet so strong,
You knew there must be something wrong.
There's nothing you can do or say,
Except look to the Lord and pray.
These unknown souls who lie with you,
What kind of labor did they do?
I know that some were kitchen hands;
Some worked with wood and some with cans;
Some dug ditches; some fixed fences,
Down where the dismal swamp commences.
With straw and mud they put together
Bricks that have withstood the weather,
And houses they built from the ground
Through all these years are still around.

Oh I'm as proud as I can be.
I know they did it all for me.
I know that I'm a better man
As on their shoulders here I stand.

I know that all the grief and pain
They bore could not have been in vain.
They lived in Faith and died in Hope
That somewhere, sometime they could cope
And find a way to make a stand
Against man's inhumanity to man.
Alas, alas, 't would not be so.
The grass upon their graves did grow.[2]

This book, which was more than fifty years in the making, was initially conceived as a family history.[3] However, as more people—both nationally and internationally—became aware of the Quanders' history, I was urged to tell the expanded story, one truly reflective of American history. This book is not another *Roots*, a fictional account based upon a slim set of facts. Instead, *The Quander Story* narrates a series of actual events that shows where we came from and who we are today. Some of the stories do not chronologically follow from what has immediately preceded. The national scope of the family history and the breadth of the family's involvement dictate that several stories are freestanding and not directly related to what has gone before or what immediately follows. As you read, the story will morph from Negro and Colored, to Black and African American, to reflect racial identification during the changing time periods.

Some readers might perceive this book as a memoir. That is not my intent, although I must take a bow or two and give myself some credit for the many years I devoted to this effort, plugging away among old dusty records in the Maryland Hall of Records in Annapolis and the Fairfax County Courthouse Archives in Virginia. One of my good friends, an Omega Psi Phi fraternity brother, said that life was too short to spend time looking back. Smart as he was, a Howard University Phi Beta Kappa, his shortsightedness has actually been an inspiration to me, setting a tone for a wider appreciation of history and how it can help or hinder us. What is history anyway? I believe history is to know, appreciate, and explain what has already occurred and to evaluate the present in the context of the past. That is exactly what *The Quander Story* seeks to do. Now it is your turn to read, enjoy, learn, savor, and share the tribulations, the triumphs, the failures and successes, and the unfolding story that is the legacy of the Quander family. Adelante!

CHAPTER 1

The Early Years
Henry Quando and
Margrett Pugg

In 1634, the *Ark* and the *Dove* landed in St. Mary's City, bringing the first White settlers to what is now Maryland. Many came in pursuit of freedom to practice their Roman Catholic faith. The new colony was founded with a 1632 land grant awarded by King Charles I of England to Cecilius Calvert, the First Lord Baltimore, and was named "Maryland" for the Catholic Mary Queen of Scots and Mary the Mother of Jesus. Although Maryland was initially intended to be a colony open to religious tolerance, those hopes were soon dashed when the growing non-Catholic majority severely restricted the right of Catholics to practice their religion.

Among those early immigrants was Henry Adams, who traveled from England to the Maryland Colony in 1639 when he was approximately twenty-two years old.[1] Adams was indentured for several years to Thomas Greene in St. Mary's County. Impoverished British emigrants could receive free passage to the New World by indenturing themselves—that is, contracting themselves to servitude, often for as long as seven years. After working off his period of indenture, Adams migrated north and, by 1650, had settled in Port Tobacco, Charles County, then the seat of the local legislature and government. As a literate, landed planter, Adams served in the legislature and Charles

County government between 1661 and 1685. He also served as a justice and a sheriff during much of this time.[2] His last will and testament, written on October 12, 1684, stated he was a widower without children and a Roman Catholic. At the time of his death, he owned eight hundred acres in Charles County.

1684 Last Will and Testament of Henry Adams, which
freed Henry Quando and Margrett Pugg in 1686

Adams's will freed two of his four enslaved, Henry Quando and
Margrett Pugg. From the earliest days of colonial America, there were
always a small number of free Blacks, as slavery had not yet emerged
as the heinous, widespread institution it later became. Some, like
Henry and Margrett, obtained their general manumission upon the
death of their owners, although the number of Blacks achieving their

freedom in this way was small compared with those who remained enslaved. The will suggests Adams had a personal relationship with Henry and Margrett. What else could his incentive have been to give the boy his own name and then to free both of them while not bestowing the same benefit on the other two slaves? Although Margrett and Henry were considerably younger than Adams, they seem to have influenced him to the extent that he not only elected to free them but also provided them with items of personal property with which they could undertake independent lives.

Henry Adams may have given the boy his own English name out of affection, but his renaming also reflected the common practice of replacing the kidnapped victims' alien African names with names the English and Irish settlers could easily relate to and pronounce. Renaming was part of the effort to subdue the slaves, to mold them as quickly as possible into subservient, docile beings that would soon have little or no recollection of their African pasts. In retrospect, however, Adams's renaming his male slave was not all bad, as the consistent use of the name "Henry," tied to the name "Quando," created a road map in documenting the Quander family's history. Occasionally, we don't know where to draw the genealogical line between one Henry and the next when there is a series of individuals, but that difficulty pales by comparison with the stability conferred by the repeated use of the name.

With the filing of Adams's will for probate on July 4, 1686, the surname "Quando" became a public record in the Americas, thus documenting for the first time the presence of the Quando/Quander family in the colony of Maryland. The Quanders are accredited as the oldest, consistently documented African American family in Maryland and possibly in all the original thirteen colonies. Many of the secrets related to the introduction of the name in this hemisphere remained hidden for centuries, only to be rediscovered in the late twentieth century, when the descendants of the present generation of Quando family members in the United States met with the descendants of the shared ancestral root, the Amaquandoh family, in Ghana in 1991.

Adams's will stated that Henry and Margrett were to be free to all intent and purposes, as though they were noe "negroes", "Also I give [unto] the said Henry Quando one flock bed and what shall belong to it, also one small chest with a Dutch lock of what shall be therein, also unto the said Margrett Pugg, one cow or calfe."[3]

They were "free," the result of a benevolent act and good intention, but released into a hostile community where Blacks were viewed as inherently inferior and presumed unable to carry out any tasks of significance. Henry and Margrett were illiterate, trapped in a strange land with a new and uncertain status, a probable loss of communication in their indigenous African languages, and no means of returning to their homeland. It is not even certain whether they were born in Maryland, Africa, or perhaps Barbados. In reality, they may not have had any other land to call home, and they elected to stay in Port Tobacco.

During the early colonial period, there was no direct slave trade between West Africa and the colonies. Rather, North American slave traders traveled to the West Indies, primarily Barbados or Jamaica, visited the slave markets, made their selections, and then put their newly acquired enslaved on ships headed north. For more than two centuries, there has passed from generation to generation of the Quander family the story of two brothers who were brought to Maryland from "the islands" and then separated, never to be reunited. Remarkably, this story has persisted in both the Maryland and Virginia branches of the family even though, with the passage of time and the expansion of distances, the later generations of the extended Quander family did not know each other.

The story suggests that in Maryland the brothers were sold to different slave owners, presumably resulting in Henry Quando going to Henry Adams and his brother passing into oblivion. "Benjamin" is the only name I have ever heard for the lost brother. The "two brothers" story relates that the children of the freed brother (Henry Quando) and the children of the still enslaved Benjamin were able to reestablish contact in Maryland and vowed never again to lose sight of their familial relationship. They clung to that relationship tenaciously through the centuries, as would be apparent at a later time.

Even less is known about Margrett Pugg Quando. Her exact year of birth is unknown, but in 1739, when she filed a petition for relief from the need to pay certain annual taxes, she gave her age as well past seventy years (this story is related later in this chapter). By that calculation, she was born earlier than 1669, which would have made her six or more years older than Henry Quando, whose birth year is believed to be 1675. No evidence has been found reflecting where or when Henry and Margrett were purchased, but later, records note Margrett as Henry Quando's wife.[4]

In 1691, when he was sixteen or seventeen years old, Henry registered his cattle mark. The Charles County registration describes the mark as a "swallow fork on both ears and underkeeled on the right ear."[5] The registration of his cattle mark would have enabled Henry to readily identify and protect his livestock and ensure that his property interests would be respected. Even at this young age, Henry exhibited an entrepreneurial spirit and a sense of self-worth.

The main industry of the area was farming. Henry and Margrett presumably were farmers, grazing their animals on whatever acreage they could secure. The farm tools bequeathed under Adams's will seemed targeted to the furtherance of farming, an occupation that would partially shield the fledgling but free Quando family from the daily racial insults and challenges of the age. Encumbered by limitations upon the ability of free Blacks to own land, the Quandos may have indentured themselves as farm hands to White settlers for the next several years, accumulating resources to help them eventually strike out on their own. In a few years, Henry's intentions to achieve independence and self-reliance were clearly manifested. On February 4, 1695, Henry, whose name was listed as "Henry Quandoo," less than nine years out of slavery, executed a ninety-nine-year freehold lease with Ignatius Wheeler, a major plantation owner in Port Tobacco, Charles County.[6] Henry's tract was 116 acres of land, part of a much larger tract called "Wheeler's Folly." The tract was just off Port Tobacco Road, a few hundred feet inside the Charles County line. The acreage was located immediately adjacent to what is now Route 301, along Mattawoman Creek. Henry's signature on the deed was an "X." Margrett was not a signatory, as women had virtually no legal rights at that time and African women had no rights at all in this hostile place. In establishing a freehold secured on a ninety-nine-year lease, Henry attained the most comprehensive, multigenerational interest that someone could hold in land, short of outright ownership. A lease of this type could be inherited by subsequent generations through 1794, the natural end of the leasehold period.

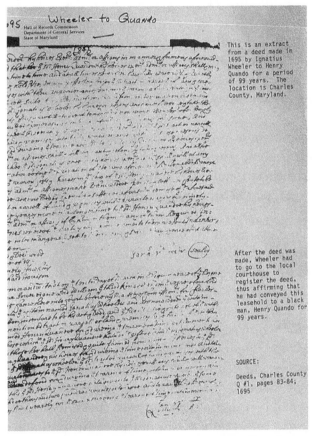

Deed from Ignatius Wheeler to Henry Quandoo, leasing
land for 99 years, Charles County, Maryland, 1695

Henry Quando probably never imagined that his securing a ninety-nine-year freehold would ever be viewed in a much larger context—that is, as a Black man taking a stand. As the holder of a freehold long-term lease, he may have enjoyed some civil freedoms despite the restrictions that were placed upon all Black residents of the county. A ninety-nine-year lease was closely akin to actual land ownership, as by definition, a freehold interest bestowed extensive rights and privileges with voting and participation in local community activities limited to landowners and freehold tenants. But did Quando ever vote or participate in community decision-making? Although institutional racism was not yet widely established, laws were being passed that restricted Black men's access to the wider community. Whether these laws translated into a denial of Henry Quando's voting and other rights is unknown, but allowing a Black man access to this level of societal participation, to help shape the direction in which his own community would proceed, is extremely doubtful.

Perhaps of more immediate importance to Henry and Margrett, gaining the freehold was their first real opportunity after manumission to put their accumulated farming skills to use on their own farm. In the ten-year period between 1686 and 1696, Henry and Margrett progressed from slavery to freedom, from dependence to self-reliance. When measured in the hostile atmosphere of their times, their advancements were monumental.

In recent times, the Quander family's history as movers and shakers for justice and social change has been recognized. Research into that history reveals that these characteristics were not recently acquired. Rather, in significant ways, this activist attitude was ably demonstrated by Henry and Margrett at a much earlier time when they recognized they could not function in this hostile land unless they actively stood up for themselves, demanding to be afforded whatever small measures of freedom were available to free Blacks in the early eighteenth century. This independent spirit and ability to earn their way was most likely exhibited during their period of servitude to Henry Adams. It is doubtful Adams would have freed them in 1686 if he thought they could not handle it. His differing attitude concerning emancipation was demonstrated by his not freeing the young male child and old woman, whom he also held in servitude, their names not even appearing in his will.

Henry and Margrett's spirit and determination to succeed in the face of adverse odds has carried over to the present. Although most of the present generation has no recollection of why this spirit is an integral part of what it is "to be a Quander," at least one example is found among the records. On June 13, 1702, Henry filed a petition before the High Court of Chancery, province and territory of Maryland, asking the court to determine whether he had to pay an annual tax that was assessed against slave owners for the privilege of having Black female slaves. His basic premise was that the tax assessment law failed to take into consideration that some of the Black women in the community were free and not profit generators for some slave owner. Moreover, Henry did not own Margrett. Henry concluded by urging that this tax law and its intended effect should be viewed as totally inapplicable to their situation.

Like other free, married women—Black or White—of her era, Margrett could not vote, own real property in her own name, or even bring suit. Moreover, women of African origin were viewed as little more than beasts of burden and a revenue-generating asset because they could produce more slaves. The court's focus seemed to be only to procure the annual provincial tax imposed upon the profits these women generated for their slave owners. The High Court of Chancery, having its own agenda to ensure that a steady stream of funds flowed into the province's coffers, ruled that the tax was to be universally levied against all Black females, whether slave or free, and directed Henry to pay up.[7]

Several valuable lessons were learned from that singular incident. First, knowing what the odds were, Henry and Margrett elected to try anyway, to contest the obvious unfairness of making a free Black man pay an annual "profit" tax on his own free wife.

Second, their contesting the issue demonstrated their strong belief that they had rights despite the refusal of the legal institutions to recognize them. Their activism dismissed any myths that our forebears, as a people, were docile, pliable, and complacent and replaced such inaccuracies with a clear statement of bold action, moving into uncharted legal waters without any known precedent or likely positive outcome.

Third, despite losing this decision, Henry and Margrett Quando continued to fight, as subsequent records show they continued to seek relief through the courts. They may not have intended their actions to be a beacon for later African Americans, but that is what resulted. They are role models of men and women in the Quander family who set a strong example of African Americans taking a stand by speaking up for their rights.

Henry's petition to the High Court of Chancery was not the only time he and Margrett stood up for themselves. My further research revealed a protracted story involving the Quando family between 1718 and 1722 that has enough twists and turns that it could be a prime time miniseries.

In 1718, a grand jury in Charles County instituted proceedings against one Ann Rannes for having a child out of wedlock.[8] Although she was referred to as a White indentured servant, the child was characterized as a mulatto. Wishing to escape the harsh treatment and public humiliation she knew was forthcoming, she sought the assistance of Thomas Wheeler, the brother of Ignatius Wheeler, who had conveyed the "Wheeler's Folly" land tract to Henry Quando in 1695. Thomas Wheeler, himself a planter as well as a bondsman, elected to prepare and sign a performance bond guaranteeing that Rannes would appear in court on the scheduled date to face the allegations of bastardizing. In the interim, he and she dreamed up a scheme they thought would create a win-win result for both of them.

Perhaps because he knew the Quando family through his brother and perhaps because he considered Rannes as a high-risk client, Thomas Wheeler persuaded Henry and Margrett's minor daughters, Mary and Elizabeth, to sign Rannes's performance bond as co-guarantors of her appearance on the assigned court date. Under the terms, the Quando sisters agreed that if Rannes failed to appear in court, they would be called to perform in her absence. Had Wheeler succeeded, the girls would have indentured themselves for seven years, probably working in Wheeler's fields. The inducement for the girls to cosign the performance bond is not reflected in the record, but presumably, they received some incentive for their agreement. Whether they understood what they were getting into is doubtful.

In all likelihood, they could not read; in fact, later records referred to their brother, Henry II, as illiterate.

Wheeler then arranged for Rannes to leave Maryland and cross the Potomac River into Virginia. It was a perfect arrangement: she would likely escape her punishment, and Wheeler would have two unpaid field hands for a seven-year duration. In the court proceedings, Wheeler portrays himself as an innocent party, someone who has been wronged by Rannes rather than conspiring with her.

This obvious setup against her daughters was not to Margrett's liking. That she and not Henry petitioned the court to stop the Wheeler-Rannes scheme strongly suggests that Henry Quando had died or was seriously ill before 1718. Margrett appeared without him on behalf of her minor daughters and petitioned the court to set aside this obvious fraud. Wheeler's ability to obfuscate caused the case to drag on for years. Moreover, the colonial courts did not sit every day. Most of the judges rode circuits and were only available to hear cases in certain geographical areas at certain times of the year. Margrett's race and gender almost assuredly contributed to the length of the case. The judges and members of the local old boy network may have assumed or simply hoped that she would give up and not pursue her petition.

But they underestimated Margrett's determination. Unlike the so-called peer group that was sitting in judgment of her and Wheeler, she knew what it was like to be a slave. She was determined that her daughters would not be indentured. It was not until June 6, 1722, almost four years after the proceedings started in *Quando v. Wheeler*, that the court fully recognized the significance of Wheeler's deceitful actions and the nature of his intentions. The deceit was set aside with a supplemental award of 2,148 pounds of tobacco to Margrett as punitive damages and costs.[9]

The victory was slow in arriving, but it must have been sweet when it was eventually realized. Margrett Quando prevailed at the trial, once again leaving a clearly defined legacy of hope and determination for successor generations to find, be inspired by, and emulate. The moral victory's returns were incalculable. The myth of the docile Negro content with his or her lot in a hostile America was once again shattered. A Black woman seeking and obtaining justice was at best a difficult task and most often a frustrated, unsuccessful effort, especially when attacking the credibility of a White male property owner of significant visibility and connections. During my research, I met Walter Ball, a direct descendant of Thomas Wheeler. Ball's research into the Wheeler family history had revealed that Thomas Wheeler—whom he called a "thief and a scoundrel"—was as deceitful, dishonest, and unreliable as his brother Ignatius Wheeler was benevolent, trustworthy, and honorable. I learned from Ball that Thomas Wheeler was regularly sued by plaintiffs alleging that he had committed some wrong against them.

Margrett's victory at the bench was short-lived. In the following year, 1723, Margrett, noted in the record as "a free 'negro' woman," was faced with a different dilemma. In that year, she filed a petition seeking relief from a tax levy that had been placed on herself and her daughters, noting as the basis of the petition her age, which was not specified, and her lack of monetary funds with which to pay the tax. The petition was denied. Margrett's financial problems suggest that successfully operating the 116-acre freehold may have been too difficult. The earnings from the Quandos' farming efforts were in all likelihood not enough to ensure a decent living and meet all expenses. Having to meet tax levies only added to the hardship.

Although the full nature of the unsuccessful 1723 petition remains clouded, Margrett's tenacious spirit set the tone for yet another legal victory. She petitioned again in 1724, this time with a fuller explanation of why she believed herself entitled to relief from the annual levy. Crucial in her petition, she sets forth that she had learned that by reason of the acts of the assembly of the province, she and her daughters were not to be taxed. Nevertheless, she has paid the taxes over time with great difficulty and seeks relief for the present (1724) and the future. The court ruled in her favor. Thus, as free persons of color, Margrett and her daughters were not required to pay the annual total levy in the amount of 616 pounds of tobacco from that date forward. No reference is noted about any refund for taxes previously collected in contradiction to the acts of the provincial assembly.

The relief obtained from the levy in 1724 proved ephemeral. Other petitions were filed in 1727, 1733, and 1739 seeking the same relief but not yielding consistent results.[10] These assessments were apparently not levied every year, but when they were, Margrett did not hesitate to seek relief from them. In her August 1733 petition on behalf of herself and her daughters, she noted that the assessments had not been sought for the prior two years. Allowed to go before the court to express herself, her petition was once again rejected. The sole reason noted was that "Margaret" Quando's claims to be "poor" and in "poor circumstances" were characterized as unproven in the record.

Henry and Margrett boldly initiated action on their own behalf. Margrett learned early that dogged persistence in pursuit of justice sometimes pays off, and she pursued relief through the courts until someone finally agreed with her. Willing to take chances and ply uncharted jurisdictional waters, they both demonstrated that African Americans were no less than other Americans and deserved a fair measure of justice and consideration. Although the victories were few and not consistently obtained, several small and successful steps were taken. The Quandos, even if unwittingly and unintentionally, laid a firm foundation to be later recognized as African American leaders.

CHAPTER 2

───────── ✦✦✦✦✦ ─────────

Bastards or Babies?

Henry and Margrett had at least four children: a son, Henry Jr., whom I'll call Henry II; and daughters Victoria, Elizabeth, and Mary. Court records show that each of their children received substantial judicial attention, most of it unfavorable. Still their legal encounters created a record for me to study and a means of painting this picture of the enduring African American legacy. Although Henry II's recognition was in business and entrepreneurship, analogous recognition was denied his sisters, at least two of whom distinguished themselves by having illegitimate children.

Having children out of wedlock was strictly forbidden. Situations in which an interracial child was born of such a relationship were dealt with most severely, although enforcement was not uniform. Even if the man and woman had strong feelings for one another, interracial marriage was not legally possible in the early eighteenth century and would be denied until the U.S. Supreme Court ruling in the 1967 landmark case *Loving v. Virginia* invalidated laws forbidding Black-White marriages.[1] Typically, when a child was born of a Black woman and a White man, the woman stood to be severely punished while the White father usually escaped any liability for his actions. In some cases, child support was required to relieve the public treasury of the need to take care of these highly scorned mulatto bastards. Conversely, if the woman was White and the man Black, both of them were harshly disciplined.

That the races were created separate and apart and should remain that way was a myth that was sorely tested.

The corollary myth that no White man in his right mind could desire a Black woman was consistently perpetuated, even though ignored whenever convenient. It was also officially unthinkable that a pure and innocent White European woman could even consider allowing herself to be touched by a licentious and lusty Black man, much less allow him to have intercourse with her. It must have been rape! In spite of these social taboos, many obviously mulatto children could be observed within just a decade or two of the introduction of Africans into Virginia in Jamestown 1619. The undisputable and marked presence of mixed-race births was the predictable result of a significant amount of sex forced on Black women by White men.

A documented example of the uneven treatment accorded to a free Black woman and a White man began in 1705. The *Court and Land Records* of Charles County report that in that year, a grand jury indicted Victoria Quando for having a child out of wedlock. She appeared in the court on January 8, 1706, and entered a guilty plea. Her sentence was ten lashes at the whipping post and a fine, which her father Henry paid on her behalf. The case reads as if having this child outside of marriage was solely Victoria's fault. No reference is made to the father's identity, but the child's racial classification as mulatto makes clear that the father was White.[2]

The frequency of the term *mulatto* tells a story in itself. I make no claim to having studied every document on the subject that appeared in the court records of the era, but I reviewed at least thirty-five documents that clearly indicated that interracial couplings were more common than the society at large cared to admit, frequently followed by the birth of mixed-race children. Such results were widely frowned upon with the all-male White judges of the courts taking it upon themselves to be the enforcers and standard setters of the public morals. Inspired by the White community's all-out effort to deter interracial sexual relationships, mulatto children were an ongoing irritant and issue of significance to the local judicial community. The determination of the Whites, generally the plantation owners themselves, to discourage lower-class Whites from having affiliations and especially sexual relations with Blacks, slave or free, caused them to monitor as closely as possible the personal behavior of their own slaves and the lesser members of Maryland society. And although it is no secret that the plantation owners were often the biggest offenders, regularly impregnating their own slaves, not all mulatto children had White fathers and Black mothers.

Although Anne Rannes had a baby by a Black man (chapter 1), far better known is the story of Eleanor "Irish Nell" Butler who in 1661 migrated to Maryland, where she was indentured to Lord Baltimore. Having fulfilled the term of her indenture, in 1681, Nell took Charles, a Black slave, as her husband (having no last name, he took the Butler surname). With the law not stabilized on the issue, Nell was forced into slavery, and all her mixed-race children were likewise born into slavery. Despite laws that forbade a legal marital union between them, I am certain that no one could convince either Nell or Charles that they were not married. Devoted, committed, and determined, their relationship and its multigenerational Butler progeny are well recognized throughout Maryland and the Washington, DC, area, and Nell and Charles are still fondly recalled today. No legal proscription could impede their personal association.

After Victoria Quando's 1706 indictment for bastardy, Henry and Margrett and their children disappear from the record books for a while. But in 1724, when Margrett was petitioning the court for tax relief, Mary Quando (sometimes referred to as "Maria Quandoe") was indicted on the same offense as Victoria.[3] The records for this period are sparse. Based on a formal complaint filed by Thomas Middleton, constable of the Piscataway Hundred, located in southern Prince George's County, a grand jury sitting in Marlborough Town accused Mary of "having [an] abase born child." The proceedings were reported as follows:

> On the fourth Tuesday in March, 1724, Maria Quandoe, having been previously summoned to court, appeared in the custody of Sheriff Thomas Middleton, and upon being confronted about the matter, stared that she would

not contend the matter, submitting herself to the
grace and mercy of the court. A decision was then
rendered by the jury that Maria should be fined
or suffer corporal punishment according to the
Act of the Assembly in such cases, provided that
if she did not pay the fine or procure anyone to
undertake to satisfy the fine for her, she was to be
then taken by Sheriff Philip Lee, Gentleman, to
the whipping post to be given on her bare body
15 lashes well laid on so that blood appears.[4]

George Hardy of Prince George's County, a carpenter, agreed to
pay to the fine. With that agreement, the matter lodged against Mary
Quando was dismissed. Hardy's action does not necessarily imply he
was the child's father. He presented himself more as a bondsman,
giving a surety to the court that the court's directed outcome would
be achieved.

However, the matter was far from over. Mary was back in court
on June 22, 1725, brought before the grand jury in the custody of
Philip Lee, sheriff. She did not contest the allegations but "humbly submit[ted] herself to the mercy of the Court."[5] Although only
fifteen months had elapsed between this case and the March 1724
proceedings, a careful reading of the two records reveals that this is a
different indictment, leading to the likely conclusion that Mary has
had another bastard child.

This time, no one stepped forward to pay the fine, and the jury
condemned Mary to a public whipping of six lashes, "well laid over
her bare back until the blood appears." The court directed Thomas
Edelene, a Prince George's County planter and the father of Mary's
child, to pay certain fees he had accrued. Edelene acknowledged
being indebted to the county in the amount of three pounds cur-
rency and pledged his property to cover the fines until paid. He was
also held bound to indemnify the residents of the county for any
charges for the maintenance and bringing up of his and Mary's bastard child. This case was unusual in that the child's White father was

identified and held accountable, although unlike Mary's whipping, Edelene's punishment was only financial.

You may wonder, considering the distinguished history of the Quander family, why I have devoted so much space to bastard children. As a student of history, I learned long ago that very few of our forebears were saints or even saintly. Many of them had high morals and good principles, but they were also human. They sustained human frailties and desires and engaged in conduct, including sexual acts, as an integral part of that human nature. Any telling of the Quander story cannot be considered truthful and balanced unless the entire story is told. That children were continually born outside of wedlock should perhaps be more attributed to the fact that their parents lacked reliable natural birth control than that they were engaging in unlawful acts. Additionally, given that many of the Quandos and other neighboring families gave birth to mixed-race babies, the attractiveness of forbidden fruit seemed to be a factor in these out-of-wedlock births. Had interracial marriage been allowed, undoubtedly, many couples would have married, and the stigma of mixed-race bastard children would never have occurred.

The Quando family's tax problems caused Margrett to appear in court regularly during this time frame. There is no evidence to show that the court appearances for unpaid taxes affected the indictments for bastardy, but one would have to wonder whether the conduct of the daughters, especially Mary for repeated illegitimate children, caused a negative pall to settle over the family.

After a brief hiatus, Mary was again before the court in *Lord Proprietary vs. Mary Quando*. In November 1727, in Upper Marlborough Town in the province of Maryland, Mary was accused by fourteen grand jurors of having another (apparently a third) "abase born child." Once again, she was brought before the court by the sheriff, Robert Tyler and, when confronted with the allegations, admitted her guilt to the court, placing herself upon their mercy. But this time, the court was tired of her repeat performances. Once again, a stern lecture was delivered about chastity, self-restraint, personal responsibility, and the immorality of repeatedly having bastard children. She met the court's admonishment with defiance of her own, refusing to divulge the paternity of the bastard child. Angered and exasperated, the court directed the maximum corporal punishment—"39 lashes well laid on so that blood appears"—plus unrecorded fees. John Winn of Prince George's County, a planter, acted as the surety and paid Mary Quando's fees to the court. There is also a reference that Mary had failed to pay previous fines, most probably assessed in her two prior bastardy cases.[6]

Even faced with this violent punishment, Mary refused to name the child's father. Although the records are comprehensive and the court dates frequent, the names of Mary's children never appear. Having three illegitimate children is not a stellar example to set for anyone, but Mary's refusal to submit to the court's insistence that she identify the father is worthy of note. But without knowing the full story, particularly whether sex between her and her children's fathers was coerced or consensual, we cannot judge with their conviction that she was a guilty sinner. And by what right do we judge? What appears on the surface may not reflect what actually occurred.

Despite incurring the ire of the authorities, Mary Quando showed a resiliency I admire, regardless of the rest of the story. Like Margrett, who regularly pursued tax relief, and Henry, who followed his own entrepreneurial spirit, Mary appeared willing to challenge the system and the status quo.

CHAPTER 3

---◆◆◆◆◆---

The Entrepreneurial Spirit Lives

Henry and Margrett Quando conveyed an inner strength to their children, a determination to succeed in the face of all odds and not let their actions be dictated by the whims of the controlling White society. These early Quanders set examples that we can respect and emulate. From 1675, when Henry Quando was born, to 1739, when Margrett obtained permanent relief from the tax levies, the family made tremendous strides. In those sixty-five years, during all which Margrett was alive, the family went from permanent slavery to freedom and the birth of four children and at least three or four grandchildren. By the late 1720s, Henry Quando II had become a businessman and entrepreneur. Although their grandchildren were bastards to the judge and local community, to the fledgling Quando family, these "abase" infants represented the next generation, an assurance there would be a future and a reason for the older family members to continue onward.

Like the rest of the family, most of what became the record of Henry II's life was played out in the context of court suits. These cases illuminate not only his creative spirit but also his determination to succeed, both characteristics he learned from his parents. Much of the family apparently still lived together during at least a portion of this time. The *List of Taxables 1733*, a list of taxable households, contained one complete "Quandoe" household living in Prince George's County that was headed by the widow Margrett and included Henry

II, Margrett Jr., Mounaca, Ann, and Viottons.[1] The infusion of new names is both confusing and illuminating. This is the first reference to a "Margrett Jr.," leading to the question of whether she was an alternate name for one of Margrett Sr.'s three daughters: Victoria, Mary, or Elizabeth. And who were Mounaca, Viottons, and Ann? Were they Margrett's grandchildren, the subjects of the bastardy proceedings held against Mary between 1724 and 1727? Was Margrett Jr. also a member of this group? The answers are uncertain. Quander family members have long wondered where the names "Mounaca" and "Viottons" came from. I have mentioned the names to several West Africans through the years and especially people from Ghana, the most likely origin of the Quando family. But no one has recognized either name or been able to provide any clues as to their origin or meaning.

The *List of Taxables 1733* also noted an Adam Quando as residing elsewhere with several other surnames listed for the location. Most likely, Adam Quando worked for this family and was thus listed at their place of residence. Later, when Henry Quando II died (c. 1742), Henry Adam H. Quando was listed as sole heir and is most probably the Adam Quando noted in the *List of Taxables 1733*.

Henry II's strong entrepreneurial spirit was cultivated through many testing events. In 1731, John Maddox filed suit in *John Maddox, Assignee, Richard Cross vs. Henry Quando* and caused a writ to be issued by the sheriff of Prince George's County to take Henry II into custody if found in his bailiwick.[2] The sheriff was directed to present Henry II to the court on the fourth Tuesday of March 1731 in Marlborough Town to answer John Maddox's charges that Henry had committed a wrongful act of trespassing upon a property, without permission, for which Maddox was entitled to recover compensation. The full nature of the alleged offense was not developed.

Henry Quando II appeared as directed. Speaking without an attorney, Henry II explained the full situation to the court, including a prior case in which he had been found entitled to attach Maddox's property to secure payment for a debt that remained unsatisfied. Having heard Henry II's side of the story, the court, in an unanticipated decision, held that Maddox, not Henry II, was the liable party. Left with no choice after this sudden turn of events, Maddox dropped his claim against Henry II. Judgment was entered against Maddox for 360 pounds of tobacco for Henry II's costs and charges for his defense of the original fraudulent suit filed by Maddox against him. Maddox pledged that his chattels and lands could be levied against by Quando to satisfy this judgment, if Maddox did not voluntarily pay the 360 pounds of tobacco. Maddox was given time to come into voluntary compliance and satisfy his debt obligation between June 1731 and July 1732. This ruling was lenient, considering that Maddox had earlier tried to cheat Henry II by claiming that he, Maddox, was the party to whom the debt was owed instead of the other way around. Alexander Frazer, acting as surety, pledged that his chattels and lands could be levied against by Henry II to satisfy the court's judgment if Maddox failed to pay the 360 pounds of tobacco within the allotted time.

But this victory would not be the swift, happy ending Henry II hoped for. A full year passed without payment of the debt obligation by either Maddox or Frazer, and Henry II had to initiate another proceeding, *Henry Quando vs. John Maddox and Richard Cross*. For this suit, Henry II was represented by Daniel Dulany, a well-respected attorney in lower Prince George's and Charles Counties. At Henry II's request, the court issued a new summons that directed Sheriff Thomas Brooks to bring John Maddox for a court hearing on the fourth Tuesday in June 1732 by reason of his failing to satisfy the debt obligation for which he was pledged by Alexander Frazer, the surety, plus costs and charges that Henry Quando II sustained in Maddox's previously filed Plea of Trespass.[3] But before the suit against Maddox could be pursued, in-person jurisdiction over Alexander Frazer had to be secured. Through Dulany, Henry II initiated a suit against Frazer in *Henry Quando vs. Alexander Frazer.*[4] The court directed Frazer to return to court on August 25, 1732, to provide information on the location of his own chattels and lands that were to be levied against for the benefit of Henry II. When Frazer failed to appear, the court entered a default against his property effective in ten days. An entry was made in the record that Quando was still owed 360 pounds of tobacco as judgment, plus an additional 238 pounds of tobacco in costs and charges incidental to the collection of the judgment.

It is not known whether Henry II ever collected his just due, by now 598 pounds of tobacco. But the key element in this story is that Henry Quando II understood and used the legal system to his advantage. Knowing the universal hostility against Blacks in Southern Maryland at the time, much credit must be given to him. He contested the denial of what he was entitled to and worked to rein in the bad actors, many of whom apparently believed they could conduct business with a Black man unfairly and with impunity, incorrectly assuming he would not oppose them, and could not win if he did.

Not many years passed before the next round of court cases, which would prove just as challenging as the Maddox and Frazer suits. Only now, Henry II faced a woman who was just as determined as he concerning a monetary obligation she owed. On November 21, 1737, Henry II made a commercial sale of linen, ladies shoes, silk handkerchiefs, tobacco, and worsted stockings, plus costs incurred incident to packing and shipping, to Miss Margorot Clements. The goods were apparently delivered to her without payment at the time of delivery. Henry II tried for several years to collect the payment, but each time, she successfully evaded paying even, according to Henry's later court petition, by marrying Samuel Clements in 1739 to escape from her debts. Incensed at her apparent indifference and further frustrated by her husband's lack of concern, Henry II, through his attorney Henry Darnall III, sued them both in the Charles County Court in 1741, alleging that in addition to a debt due to him by Margorot Clements, her conduct constituted fraud. He asked for a judgment of 852 pounds of tobacco, plus another 852 pounds of tobacco (i.e., 1,704 pounds as double indemnification). Seeking a double return was the most direct method for handling and punishing the commission of fraud.

On June 9, 1741, Margorot and Clements filed an answer to Henry's suit, and a full twelve-man jury trial was held. William Clements Sr., whose relationship to Samuel Clements is unknown, pledged land and cattle as security for the debt claimed due in the event that Margorot and Samuel were convicted and did not either pay the debt or submit to possible incarceration in debtors prison.

Henry II won! This all-White jury upheld the suit of a Black man who was struggling for right in a country that respected no rights for the descendants of Africans. Judgment was entered for Henry II for 852 pounds of tobacco plus 2,129 pounds of tobacco awarded for his costs. Winning another suit surely was a great moral and psychological victory for him, and it should have been a financial victory as well. But Samuel Clements seemed to have a habit of not paying. In a new suit only two months later, on August 11, 1741, Henry II alleged that on March 1, 1738, he contracted with Clements to build a 12x16-foot house in exchange for 500 pounds of tobacco, but now three years later, he remained unpaid. Acting on Henry II's behalf, Attorney Henry Darnall III demanded judgment of 1,000 pounds of tobacco, which was awarded, plus 482 additional pounds of tobacco to cover Henry II's costs.[5]

Whether Henry II was able to collect on the favorable judgments seems doubtful. He died in debt in 1742. Prince George's County records reflect that Henry II owned a mare, a colt, broad axes, carpentry tools, a green rug, a blue rug, assorted wearing apparel, five undescribed mementos, and other small items of little value. The estate's estimated value was 11.6 pounds sterling, considerably less than the 50 pounds sterling he owed at his death.[6] Although Henry II is described as a "planter" in the August 11, 1741, Charles County Court records the inventory of his estate does not mention the ninety-nine-year freehold, the most valuable asset, leading me to suspect that the 116 acres of the lease had been returned to the Wheeler family. Given the tax problems the family had struggled with for years, it would be no surprise if the freehold failed to pay county taxes. Or perhaps it was reclaimed by the Wheelers due to the Quandos' inability to meet their periodic rent obligation for the freehold.

Although Henry Quando II's illiteracy may have impaired his ability to move about provincial Maryland society as freely as a literate Black man of his nature might have been able to, his actions paint a vivid picture of a man who did considerably more than many of his peers of any color. The entrepreneurial spirit lived in Henry

Quando II! Records describe him as a planter. The suit with Margorot Clements suggests he was a dry goods retailer. Although the tobacco he sold her was surely grown and processed locally, the linen, ladies shoes, silk handkerchiefs, and worsted stockings had to have been secured elsewhere, perhaps in Baltimore, Philadelphia, New York, or even England. His building of the small house for Samuel Clements suggests he was a skilled carpenter. Most significantly, he persevered in his use of the legal system to claim justice, thus asserting that he had rights equal to all other Maryland provincials to seek redress in the court and to have debts owed to him paid in the same way Whites in the community expected obligations to be honored. His consistently standing up for his rights left a blueprint for all of us who came after him.

CHAPTER 4

$\cdot\;\cdot\;\blacklozenge\blacklozenge\blacklozenge\blacklozenge\cdot\;\cdot\;\cdot$

The Quander Family
Seems to Disappear

In spite of my diligent research, the many historical records up to the *List of Taxables 1733* that had depicted the Quando family triumphs and tribulations suddenly seemed to dry up, and I am frustrated by having to relate the story with an apparent break in continuity. The lack of records may be partially explained by a lack of lawsuits. In addition, Henry and Margrett Quando had only one son, which made it likely that only his children carried the Quando name. Henry Quando II also left only one son we know of, Henry Adam H. Quando III. After the inventory of Henry II's estate was completed in 1744, only one document citing a Quando appears until the Second Decennial U.S. Census of 1800.

On June 17, 1776, Humall Godfrey, Elisha Harrington, and Robert Wade of Prince George's County filed a performance bond of two hundred pounds sterling for the estate of Margaret Godfrey Quando.[1] In subsequent proceedings, Henry Quando is listed as her sole heir and next of kin, although their exact relationship is undetermined. Whether this Margaret is the "Margrett Jr." listed in the *List of Taxables 1733* is unknown but possible, Robert Wade was listed as residing in the same residence as Adam Quando in the same *List of Taxables*.

With the exceptions of the estate documents connected to Henry Quando II in 1744 and Margaret Godfrey Quando in 1776, the Quando family disappeared from the written records of Prince George's County until the U.S. Census of 1800, which lists a "Henry Quander, free Negro." The appearance of this fourth Henry confirms a naming pattern that had persisted since at least 1684, from Henry Adams (1684) to Henry Quando (1684–c1718), Henry Quando II (1731–1742), Henry Adam H. Quando III (1742), and Henry Quander IV (1800). The 1800 U.S. Census also shows a Nancy Quanders as the head of a household of three persons then residing in the District of Columbia. Who was this Nancy Quanders? Where did she come from, and how does she fit into the Quander equation? These are questions to which I still have no answers.

Why the Quando/Quander family was completely missed in the First Decennial U.S. Census, conducted in 1790, remains a mystery. After the U.S. Census of 1800 documented two Quander households, one each in Prince George's County and the District of Columbia, subsequent census records show very few Quanders. The family was generally not reflected in the 1810 Census (although a major portion of the tracts of this census was destroyed during the War of 1812) or the U.S. Censuses for 1820, 1830, or 1840 conducted in Maryland, the District of Columbia, or Virginia. The Quander family's continued presence in the region makes it is difficult to understand how they were excluded in the decennial count so consistently. Fortunately, the plethora of other available documents—such as tax records and land transactions showing Quander interactions with people in Maryland, Virginia, and later Washington, DC—supports the Quander family history.

The Quander story takes up indirectly in June 1799 when retired President George Washington directed that an inventory of his enslaved be taken at his eight-thousand-acre Mount Vernon plantation. As a young man, Washington assumed the societal values of his day, taking the institution of slavery in stride. Although Virginia laws restricted the importation of slaves purchased elsewhere, Washington learned early that he could purchase perhaps three slaves in Maryland for the price of two in Virginia. Despite the Virginia restriction on importing slaves, Washington offered a reward in the Maryland *Gazette* on August 20, 1761, for the apprehension of four runaway slaves whom he had purchased in Maryland and brought into Virginia. This bold public advertisement suggested Washington was more concerned about the prompt return of his property than he was about being charged with evading a Virginia tax law.

But in the coming decades, as Washington matured, serving as a colonel during the French and Indian Wars in the 1760s and later as commander of the armed forces in the Revolutionary War, his thinking slowly changed, and he soured on the institution of slavery. Even as early as the 1760s and even more so in the 1770s, his diaries and letters clearly showed he contemplated freeing his slaves. He tried to get several of his prominent fellow Virginians—among them Thomas Jefferson, James Madison, and George Mason—to do the same. They declined mostly because of the tremendous economic loss they would sustain if they lost their slaves' free labor. Unable to solicit their support, he resolved to do at least some small measure himself and elected to purchase no more slaves after 1774.

Washington noted in his diary that as many of his "servants" were skilled artisans, they could earn a living if they were freed. He even worked on a plan to rent out four of Mount Vernon's five farms and retain only Mansion House Farm where he resided. Because he could not get the desired cooperation from his famous Virginia neighbors and after he accepted the demands of running the newly created federal government, the diary entries indicate that the plan never reached the point of implementation. Only from these diary entries and various letters he wrote or received are we aware that Washington was trying to end slavery by setting an example to persuade the other powerful men of his era to do the same.

Washington's reflections suggest he was influenced by the 1776 Declaration of Independence and the 1787 Constitution and the idealistic statements in those documents concerning liberty, justice, and domestic tranquility. Likewise, it is well established that he was greatly moved by the honorable participation of the several thousand African Americans who served in the Revolutionary War. Claiming belief in statements about liberty and equality and the fraternity of humankind while ignoring the cries of hundreds of thousands of Blacks, both slave and free, was the worst hypocrisy. Washington understood that to continue to deny Black men and women their birthright was wrong and demeaning. In his last will and testament of 1792, he provided for the emancipation of his own slaves upon his death and for the care and annual monetary allotments for the former slaves in their old age. His estate remained open into the 1830s in order to care for the last of this group.

In December 1800, a year after Washington's death, his wife Martha freed his enslaved and released the current generation of her own slaves, many of whose relatives came to Mount Vernon with her when she married in 1759. The consequences of Martha Washington's action shifted the Quander story from being exclusively a Maryland story to becoming a Virginia and District of Columbia story too. Among those slaves scheduled to be freed were Sukey Bay and her daughters Nancy and Rose Carter.[2] From documents created in the 1830s, we know Nancy survived. Her marriage to Charles Quander, probably in about 1810, lets us pick up the story of the Quander family. This is the first time we see the Quander name in Virginia, which suggests Charles came from the Maryland side of the Potomac River. The area where the family lived was a short distance from where the river is less than a mile wide. Charles Quander was "a free man of color," which in the parlance of the day meant he was neither enslaved nor White. He was most likely one of the direct lineal descendants of Henry Quando, although I could find no confirming records.[3] The couple had at least three children: Gracee (born c. 1811), Elizabeth Quander Hayes (born c. 1815), and Osmond Quander (born c. 1825). Osmond would later be recorded in the Fairfax County, Virginia, land records as a free Negro landowner of more than three hundred acres.[4]

In 1793, the Virginia General Assembly enacted legislation "to restrain the practice of 'negroes' going at large." The preamble to this legislation stated that "great inconveniences have arisen from the practice of hiring 'negroes' and mulattoes, who pretend to be free, but are in fact slaves." To correct this problem, the state required that "every free 'negro' or mulatto" was required to register with the clerk of the court in the city or county where he or she resided. The registrant was required to specify his or her name, age, color, and stature by whom and in what court the said "negro" or mulatto was emancipated or that the said "negro" or mulatto was born free.[5]

As a result of this demeaning legislation, the present generation of the Quander family is blessed with registration records that let us know with some certainty who several of our forebears were, what they looked like, when they were born, and under what circumstances they obtained their freedom. Although it is repugnant that human beings should be required to register themselves like prize cattle so that Whites would know who the free Blacks were and what they were up to, these registrations are a rich trove of information available to all African Americans seeking to learn more about their families.

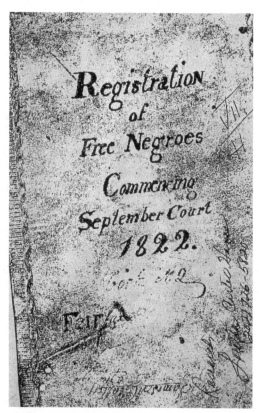

Cover, Registration of Free Negroes, Volume II and III,
Fairfax County, Virginia, which listed several Quanders

Misplaced for decades, the second two volumes of the three-volume *Registration of Free Negroes for Fairfax County* were discovered in January 1974 in the attic of the Fairfax County Courthouse. Volume I, 1790–1822, has not been located. It is speculated that it was either destroyed or remains hidden within some family's ancestral private papers. Dirty and water-stained, the books were recognized as the treasure they were and were immediately photocopied to ensure against recurring loss, damage, or theft. Volume II covers 1822 to 1835. Volume III covers 1835 to 1861, the last entry being made on April 15, 1861, just two days before Virginia seceded from the Union.

For virtually all the Virginia Quander family members, each registration included the age, height, scars, and other marks of each registrant. If the registrant was freeborn, in most cases, the name of that person's mother is also included. If a slave owner freed the registrant, then generally, the name of the freeing owner is listed. Occasionally, a Caucasian who filed the registration on behalf of the registrant would list not only the emancipated person but also name that person's mother as well, thus expanding the historic information for two or more generations.

The individual registers of free Blacks verify the continued presence and diversity of the Quander family and related family members for the period as well as attesting to the family's presence in Fairfax County during the earlier information-starved years. Register No. 23, Vol. III, describes Elizabeth Quander Hayes:

> The bearer hereof Elizabeth Hayes, four feet five and a half inches high, about Twenty-one years of age of a dark Complexion, a scar on the right Cheek prominent features, considerably marked with the Small pox is the daughter of Nancy Quonder who was emancipated by Gen. George Washington, as appears by the Certificate of Dennis Johnston, Esq. this day filed in my office. Whereupon and c. Given under my hand this 17th day of October, 1836. [Signed] Tho.

Moss October Court 1836 Examined by the
Court.

This entry not only describes Elizabeth Quander Hayes's short,
dark, pocked appearance, but also it identifies Nancy Quander
("Quonder") as Elizabeth's mother. But the information provided
is far more illuminating as the reference to Dennis Johnston adds
another dimension to the family history. At a later time, Johnston
would be noted in various records as the owner of Charles Henry
Quander (c. 1845–1919), dairy farmer, as well as other Quander
enslaved who would be reflected in District of Columbia and
Maryland records.

Besides Elizabeth, there were nine other Quander registrations
(some duplicates or for other time periods) included in the Fairfax
registers, including two references to Charles Quander (not the
Charles married to Nancy); Gracee (Elizabeth's sister); Julia; Lewis
(Gracee's son); Nancy; and Orza (which apparently refers to Nancy's
son, Osmond). The Quander registers generally follow the pattern of
the Elizabeth Quander Hayes registration given above.

In addition to born Quander family members, the registers
have proved helpful in providing information about several people
who married into the family (e.g., Letty Carter, who later married
Osmond Quander) or were well-known lineal ancestors of Quanders
(e.g., West Ford). Register No. 287 describes Letty as follows:

The Bearer hereof Letty Carter a woman of
colour, dark brown complexion, four feet eight
inches high about twenty-two years of age, a mole
or natural mark on the right cheek, a deep scar or
hole near the same, and a scar on the inside of
the left arm occasioned by a burn is the daughter
of Joe and Cornelia Carter free persons of colour
and born free, as appears from the affidavit of
James Potter and Levi Burke on file in my Office.
Whereupon &c. Oct. Ct. 1849 Examd. by the
Court.

West Ford, who was the grandfather or great-grandfather of several Quànder family members, appears in two registers.[6] He is described in Register No. 121, Book II as follows:

> Virginia to wit: The bearer hereof West Ford a yellow man about forty seven years of age five feet eight and an half inches high pleasant countenance, a wrinkle resembling a scar on the left cheek, a scar on the left corner of the upper lip, is a free man emancipated by the last Will and Testament of Hannah Washington as appears from an original Register heretofore granted by the County Court of Fairfax and this day surrendered the said West Ford has with him two children one a boy by the name of Daniel with a scar in his forehead about fourteen years of age the other a Girl about eleven years of age, the children of Priscilla Ford a free woman manumitted by Isaac McPherson, as appears by a certificate of George C. Washington on file in my office. Whereupon &c. Given under my hand this 17th day of October 1831.

In addition to the wealth of information generated by the 1793 law requiring free Blacks to register, Quander family history gained as a result of two other laws. In 1806, the state legislature adopted a law that required all freed slaves to leave Virginia. This later law partially contradicted the 1793 law requiring registration. Neither law was consistently enforced, but like the earlier law, records related to the 1806 law requiring free Blacks to leave Virginia also supply valuable information. In the 1850s, as the number of free Negroes began to significantly increase, there was a surge of petitions from free Blacks to remain in Virginia.[7] Typical are the 1853 petitions of brothers Charles and Philip Quander who were allowed to remain in the county.

The records produced as a result of a third law added even more to the Quander saga. On April 16, 1862, the U.S. Congress adopted "An Act for the Release of Certain Persons Held to Service or Labor in the District of Columbia," which freed approximately 3,100 slaves residing in the District. Their former owners were allowed to file petitions for monetary compensation for the loss of slave labor, apparently the only instance in which slaveholders received any compensation for the loss of their enslaved.

Two of those former slaves for whom compensation was sought were George Quander and Ned Quander. Dennis Johnston petitioned on July 14, 1862, on behalf of himself and other heirs of Francis Johnston, deceased, claiming entitlement to compensation for the service and labor of George and Ned Quander, referred to as "persons of African descent." Noting that the two Quander men were now discharged from all claim of the petitioner, Johnston further stated

> that at the time of said discharge the said George Quander was of the age of 39 years, about 5 feet, 8 inches high, brown and heavy made, and the said Ned Quander was of the age of 37 years, brown, short and delicate in appearance. That your petitioner acquired his claim to the aforesaid service or labor of the said George Quander and Ned Quander by the decease of Francis Johnston [illegible word] who owned them for more than thirty years, that your petitioner's claim for the service or labor of said George Quander and Ned Quander, was at the time of said discharge therefrom, of the value of fourteen hundred dollars each in money.

> Your petitioner hereby declares that he bears true faithful allegiance to the government of the United States, and that he has not borne arms against the United States in the present rebellion, nor in any way given aid or comfort thereto.

It is well known in our family that Charles Henry Quander, dairy farmer and grandfather of Gladys Quander Tancil (1921–2002), was also the former slave of Dennis Johnston, whose family resided on a large plantation in the Hayfield area of Fairfax County.[8] Gladys remembers as a young child of five years of age, in 1926, being driven past the site and hearing her Aunt Lizzy (Elizabeth Jane Quander, 1888–1968) comment, "This was the plantation where my daddy was a slave. When he stopped back here, he'd often say, 'I'm going back home for a visit.'"

In Johnston's 1862 petition, George and Ned Quander were listed as being thirty-nine and thirty-seven years old respectively and therefore would have been born in about 1823 and 1825. Although the exact year of Charles Henry's birth is not known, based upon other informational sources, he was born in the early to mid-1840s, as he was in his mid to late seventies when he died in 1919. Under this time line, either George or Ned could have been Charles Henry's father.

No one in the Johnston family bothered telling Charles Henry about President Lincoln's Emancipation Proclamation, which was effective January 1, 1863. Eventually, he heard about it, but having no place to go, Charles Henry remained at the Hayfield plantation to all appearances remaining in servitude to the Johnston family. However, in 1867, he finally decided he had had enough. He announced to the Johnstons that he was aware slavery had ended and that he was now leaving. Not wishing to lose his future years of service and potential labor, he being a young man in his twenties in the prime of his working ability, the Johnstons asked him to remain and agreed to pay him. Charles Henry accepted the offer for compensation and received a lump sum for his years of uncompensated

Charles Henry Quander (c1843-c1919), grandfather of Gladys Quander Tancil, seated on wagon at Quander Road dairy farm, c1915

51

service between 1863 and 1867. After he obtained the money, he quit working for the Johnston family, although they maintained a cordial relationship.

Charles Henry was illiterate, but he was steeped in common sense. He purchased land soon after obtaining the lump sum from the Johnstons and, over the decades, accumulated at least eighty-eight acres along Route One in Fairfax County, not far from Fort Hunt Road. His land was not in a single parcel, although several acquisitions were adjacent, creating larger tracts. Other parcels were spread about the immediate area. In the late 1870s through the early 1880s, he obtained much of the acreage surrounding the historic Spring Bank manor house, which had been built in the early nineteenth century by George Mason VI (1786–1834), grandson of George Mason IV, author of the Virginia Declaration of Rights. Charles Henry turned the land into a successful dairy farm, and Gladys's Aunt Lizzy ran it for more than forty years after Charles Henry's death in 1919. Gladys finally closed the dairy in 1964.

Charles Henry did not purchase the land directly from George Mason VI but rather from a Mr. and Mrs. Downey. Mrs. Downey is reputed to have said that she much preferred having her two sons play with the local colored children than associating with the poor Whites in the area. This phenomenon was not unknown in Southern communities, where Whites and Blacks lived in the same neighborhoods. Typically, the young children of both races played together, although their education was segregated. When the White children were twelve or thirteen years old, their parents separated them socially as well. Gladys remembered an occasion years later when Bruce Downey, the younger son, visited her grandfather's house. The two men, both then well over seventy years of age, hugged and had a long, warm visit, remembering their childhoods and sharing with each other their lives in the intervening fifty years.

The legacy of Charles Henry Quander remains with us Quanders today, as we are all far richer in our personal lives as a result of his having passed this way. Not just his children and grandchildren have benefited, as each of us in some measure has come to appreciate what he and other Quanders of his generation accomplished and achieved. Like Henry and Margrett Quando and Henry Quando II, Charles Henry Quander took advantage of every opportunity that came his way, however small, and made something from nothing.

CHAPTER 5

Quanders, Clagetts, and a Walnut Tree

Court records continued to chronicle the Quander family in the nineteenth century, sometimes as upstanding citizens, sometimes not. The stories I include here are typical of Quander family history and, I am certain, the histories of many African American families whose stories lie hidden in forgotten newspaper articles and court and civil documents. Although the Quander intersection with George Washington will always stand out, the case of *Quando v. Clagett* is perhaps the best example of how Quando/Quander history and American history have intersected.[1] Before this demand for freedom was over, Francis Scott Key, the famed patriot and author of "The Star-Spangled Banner," would serve as Quando's lawyer in a major legal matter that also involved William Marbury, the famous plaintiff attorney in *Marbury v. Madison* and chief judge of the District of Columbia.[2]

Many years ago when my interest in the family history reached a fever pitch, I undertook to examine as many publications as I could find that were relevant to local history. In the late 1970s, in an index of nineteenth-century court cases, I was surprised to find *Quando v. Clagett*, a case decided by the circuit court of the District of Columbia on May 14, 1830. Who was Clagett, and who was this person identified in the record as "Negro Harry Quando?" Was he one of the descendants of the family still enslaved in Prince George's County? And why was he identified as "Quando" while the rest of the family was using the updated "Quander" spelling?

For several years, I was a member of the board of trustees of the Accokeek Foundation, which oversees the operation of the National Colonial Farm, located in the Piscataway Park, Maryland. As a board member, I was delighted to make the acquaintance of author and historian Brice M. Clagett, a prominent attorney, who was then completing a history of his sector of the Clagett family. Brice had only heard of *Quando v. Clagett*, but he contacted a cousin, John H. Clagett IV, an archivist at the National Archives. Suddenly, Negro Harry Quando came to life, putative spouse and several children included. With John's assistance, I learned about Miss Margaret Clagett whose final last will and testament read in part as follows:

> After my decease, it is my will that my woman Maria and all her increase including the children that she now has to be free and manumitted forever and the money that is now due me to be received by Thomas Clagett and for the support of the said Maria and her children until the last of May next. I also desire that my woman Rhoda and all her increase to be free and manumitted after serving the term of two years where Elizabeth Osborn shall hire her anywhere in the district and the hire to be applied to the getting of said children good places and paying Elizabeth Osborn for her trouble. My will is that my man Harry is to serve one year to any person that will give a fair hire for him one half to be applied to the support of Maria and her children and the other part to himself in witness whereof I set my hand and affix my seal in presence of the subscribing witness this twenty-ninth day of December 1823.[3]

Miss Clagett's directive that half of Harry's wages "be applied to the support of Maria and her children" suggests a familial relation. I believe they were a family and that Margaret Clagett wanted to be reasonably assured they would continue as a family unit after her death.

Because Miss Clagett had not named an executor, the Prince George's County Court presumably appointed one. Based on a summons he received five years later, I surmise that James Clagett, another cousin, was appointed to serve. In 1830, District of Columbia Chief Judge William Cranch summoned James Clagett to appear before the circuit court to answer the petition of "Henry Quandil," which had been filed against Clagett.

Miss Clagett only referred to her slave as "my man Harry," never stating a surname. When the case was initiated, the handwriting style indicated that her man's name was not Harry but Henry and that his surname was Quandoe. I examined the document with a magnifying glass, and whether the name was *Henry* or *Harry* was still unclear. When the official proceedings were published in *Reports of Cases Civil and Criminal in the United States Circuit of the District of Columbia* (1801–1841), the name of the petitioner was Negro Harry Quando, and the case was entitled *Quando v. Clagett*. I have followed the court's use of *Harry*. But there can be no doubt. Whether his given name was Harry or Henry and whether his surname was Quando, Quandoe, or Quandil, it is the same person.

Miss Clagett's cousin Thomas Osbourn visited the register on October 25, 1825, to certify that he was a witness to her will and signature. As the will was dated December 29, 1823, she almost surely died between then and October 25, 1825. I reviewed five certificates of freedom issued after her death. From the certificates, it emerged that Miss Clagett's directions to free her slaves were followed inconsistently. Rhoda Glasgow's manumission appears to have been effected promptly.[4] She was to be freed after serving two years after Miss Clagett's death, and her manumission was certified by Trueman Tyler, Register of Wills for Prince George's County, on October 13, 1827. The same delayed freedom did not apply to "Maria and all of her increase," as the provision was that she and her children were to be manumitted upon Miss Clagett's death. However, the records indicate that Maria and her three daughters (Mary Ellen, age eighteen; Nancy, age seventeen; and Susannah Jones, age sixteen) were not certified for freedom until the same date Rhoda received her freedom.

Aware that Miss Clagett's will provided for his freedom after a year of compensated service, Harry must surely have been waiting for instructions of when to proceed to the courthouse to secure his certificate of freedom. He knew freedom for Maria and her daughters has been delayed two years. He waited for several years after that, presumably inquiring as well as any enslaved Black man could regarding James Clagett's inaction concerning Miss Clagett's will. As months grew into years, did Harry Quando become restless, perhaps even despondent, about his fate? Or did he become angry? His frustration may have been local knowledge, and someone may have urged him to pursue the matter in court. To do so would require taking legal action against a White man. That Harry did not petition the court until four or five years after he should have been freed suggests he considered his suit a serious, and possibly dangerous, action. The stakes were high, and a favorable outcome was far from assured.

How Harry secured legal counsel is not known, but on January 4, 1830, Francis Scott Key filed a petition for freedom on his behalf. The petition states "humbly that [Harry Quando] is a free man and is unjustly held in bondage by a certain James Clagett. Whereupon, he prays that a subpoena may be issued to the said Clagett that he may appear and answer hereto and that your Petitioner may be discharged."[5] On that same day, the court placed the case on the calendar for a trial and issued a summons to James Clagett to appear before the circuit court of the District of Columbia to answer the petition filed against him.

The estate retained William Marbury as counsel. Marbury asserted that Margaret Clagett only intended for Rhoda and Maria, plus their children, to obtain their freedom under her will. He contended that the language of the will relating to Harry stated only "that my man Harry is to serve one year to any person that will give a fair hire for him one half to be applied to the support of Maria and her children and the other part to himself" and said nothing concerning his freedom after he completed the year of hired service. Marbury maintained that "having specifically used proper words of emancipation in regard to her other slaves and omitted them in Harry Quando's case, the testator must have intended to manumit the former [Rhoda and Maria and their children] only." On the basis of this lack of specific language that Harry Quando was to be freed, the estate demurred on freeing him.

On May 14, 1830, the court issued its decision in *Quando v. Clagett*, holding there could be no doubt of the intention of the testatrix, Miss Clagett, to emancipate the petitioner, Harry Quando. The whole object of her will evidently was the emancipation of her slaves. Marbury's legal position, as noted in the court's comments, was found to be without merit.

The case was over! The victory was won! A legal precedent had been established. But just as Quando burst onto the scene in 1830, he likewise departed. What happened to him after he gained his freedom is anybody's guess. I never found any later reference to him in Maryland, Virginia, or Washington, DC. Despite his hasty exit from history's stage, his legacy of standing up for what was rightfully his, in spite of possible retaliation, is left with us to study and appreciate and to recognize as the significant and moral contribution he made in the face of adversity. *Quando v. Clagett* underscores many of the principles that have carried the Quander family successfully through many literal trials, tribulations, and then successes. Looking back to Henry Quando and his wife, Margrett Pugg, you observe a certain spirit of determination that carried them through dark hours. Seeing the same determination from Harry Quando 146 years after the first documented presence of the Quando family in 1684 is nothing short of an inspiration. Ever since I discovered *Quando v. Clagett* and recognized the involvement of the famous Key and Marbury participants, I have had a sense that this entire scenario was a sacred unfolding of a historical event, something that was intended to be found, a valuable moral lesson that tells us to never, never give up for what is right and just. Although Harry Quando's life after 1830 may be forever unknown, what he left us with is priceless. He showed how a Black man could successfully challenge the established system and prevail, seemingly against all odds. And for that contribution to American history and the history of the Quander family, we will forever remain in his debt.

Although we don't know what happened to Harry Quando, the story of the Quanders and Clagetts was not yet finished. On October 9, 1875, Henry Waring Clagett of Mount Pleasant Estate in Prince George's County executed a deed for over an acre of land and a small house to freedman John Henry Quander (c. 1827–1890s), also of Prince George's County, in exchange for $575. This sale made John Henry Quander one of the first African American owners of real property in the county. In 1988, the property, located on Old Crain Highway in Upper Marlboro, Maryland, was placed on the Register of Historic Sites for Prince George's County.[6] In the same year, the Maryland National Capital Park and Planning Commission (M-NCPPC) also identified the Quander property and noted its historic significance. The M-NCPPC report describes the history of property ownership as follows:

> Before the Civil War, a dwelling had been erected on the south side of that lane [Mount Pleasant Lane], the home of Henry Waring Clagett, one of the heirs of the Waring Family's Mount Pleasant Estate. Clagett's house no longer stands. The lane remains a private road (Mount Pleasant Road) and leads past a tiny one-and-one-half story frame dwelling (3708 Old Crain Highway), built before 1875 by freedman John Henry Quander, and deeded to him by Henry Waring Clagett.[7]

The statement "built before 1875 by freedman John Henry Quander" is illuminating. No other information has been uncovered to date that reveals who built the house and when it was constructed. Older Quander family members told me the house was already on the property when John Henry Quander acquired title in 1875.

Henrietta Quander Walls, the last family member to reside there, vacated the home in about 1988. Although much of the early history of the property and the house remains sketchy, Susan G. Pearl, a research historian with the M-NCPPC's Historic Preservation Section, assembled and synthesized valuable information illuminating a significant presence of African Americans and the Quanders in particular in Prince George's County. She verified that Henry Waring Clagett lived just north of the site in Marlboro Meadows and owned extensive properties in the immediate vicinity. Although it is not known whether Clagett and Quander had a business relationship, such as employer-employee for farming any of the nearby fields, some sort of relationship is implied by the relocation of John Henry, his wife Henrietta, and their seven children from Mordecai Plummer's Poplar Ridge plantation where they had been enslaved to a site purchased directly from Clagett. Subsequently, the Quander family had a multigenerational relationship with the Clagett family, including several Clagetts who were the family attorneys. Additionally, Quanders have African American Clagett blood relatives who are themselves alleged to be the slave era descendants from the White Clagetts.

In 1996, Susan Pearl and M-NCPPC published the *African-American Heritage Survey*, which provides details on 107 individual properties, including residences, churches, cemeteries, schools, and fraternal lodges, associated with African Americans in Prince George's County. This publication refers to the Quander house as a "rare example of a post-Civil War freedman's dwelling," one of the few surviving dwellings erected by the newly freed people during the Reconstruction period.[8] Several generations of Quanders were born in this modest little house, which originally had a small living room and dining room on the first floor and two bedrooms upstairs. The original kitchen was in a separate little structure. After it burned, a new kitchen and a porch were added to the back of the house. The house never had running water. Everyone used an outhouse and well, with a water pump on the outside, just off the kitchen. The house was heated with oil, and propane gas was used for cooking. It was finally wired for electricity in the 1950s.

Although the property was small, at various times, the Quanders grew corn, tobacco, and vegetables and kept chickens, pigs, and milk cows. The family also maintained riding and carriage pulling horses. Some of the vegetables were sold in town, but the animals were for personal use or consumption.

Family members recall an expansive, heavily canopied walnut tree that grew behind the house that everyone admired. Even on the hottest days of summer, it was always cooler under the tree because of its deep shade. When the weather permitted, the family would sit under the tree to talk and relax from chores. Homework was completed, and picnics were enjoyed. The walnut tree presided over family weddings and Sunday dinners. Through the years, the Quanders also hosted many buffets for school, beneficial societies, and colored Catholic or Republican political and community events. All these gatherings were held in the yard, and always, there was a table laden with food under the walnut tree.

In retrospect, some of these gatherings were historical occasions. Many meetings of different organizations were held at the Quander home that influenced later events. For example, some of the early discussions that resulted in the 1880 creation of the St. Mary's Colored Beneficial Society were held here. Later, after the society had built its own hall in 1892, committee meetings, picnics, and Sunday suppers continued to be held at the Quander property under the walnut tree. The same can be said for various activities related to the Knights of St. John Commandery #74, the Colored Catholics, and St. Mary's school, all which were rigidly segregated at the time. Pearl located a record that referred to my great-grandfather, Gabriel Quander (1857–1893), as one of a group of men appointed to a committee in 1892 to undertake the planned construction of a new school for the colored children in Upper Marlboro. It is believed some of the planning meetings took place at the homestead, again under the old walnut tree.

Many people wanted to buy the huge walnut tree and cut it down to make furniture. However, William Domonic Quander (1870–1940) would never dream of cutting the tree down. (Domonic and Gabriel Quander, my great-grandfather, were brothers.) The tree gave plenty of nuts, which were used for cooking, especially desserts, and given away to family and friends. Eventually, portions of the tree had to be cut down due to disease and its own heavy weight. Later, Domonic's daughter Henrietta was forced to cut down the entire remaining tree. It was like a death in the family. Many of their best family memories were associated with activities and events that occurred under the old walnut tree. Moreover, that tree was witness to some of the most important events related to African Americans in Prince George's County.[9]

After 115 years in the family, the house was sold in 1990 as the final component of the estate of William Domonic Quander. It was purchased by the Chapman family, the Caucasian next-door neighbors and longtime associates of the Quander family. Their long-range plans for the house and the site are unknown. Because the site is registered as one of Prince George's County historic sites, any changes to the house or property will have to be executed in compliance with county regulations. Unfortunately, the house has remained vacant, and the site is neglected, subject to what historians call "demolition by neglect."

CHAPTER 6

Felix Quander
Negro Thief or Honorable Man?

Not everyone blazes a trail like Negro Harry Quando or landowning freedman John Henry Quander. In every family, there are a few relatives who instead burn bridges and light destructive fires. One such ancestral relative in the Quander family was Felix Quander (born c. 1827), who was notorious for his frequent brushes with the law. More than 140 years have passed since Felix made his splash, and family members still talk about him. Several years ago, I assembled an exhibit about Felix based on the many newspaper articles of his time that chronicled his escapades. I was fascinated with the story they wove and shared it with various groups, especially during Black History Month. Audiences relish my talk about Felix and his problems, played out in the post-Reconstruction atmosphere of 1879 as the political and economic environment of the time unfolded, warts and all, through this series of articles.

Felix was the second son of Gracee Quander and an unknown father and the grandson of Charles Quander and Nancy Carter Quander. The earlier part of Felix's story is based on Fairfax County Court minutes; his later story rests on about fourteen newspaper articles that appeared in 1879 that detailed the trials, tribulations, and near death of Cousin Felix. In retrospect, many of Felix's problems rooted, though they were in the prevailing racist attitudes of his time, also reflected the beliefs of his contemporaries, even members of his own family, that he was a man who courted trouble.

Lewis Quander (c1821-1864), grandson
of Nancy Carter Quander and Charles
Quander and brother of Felix Quander

The story begins in August Court 1868 when Felix, his wife Julia, and their son Joseph were accused of having committed assorted charges of trespass and assault, one of many such brushes with the law.[1] A grand jury of seventeen men issued a true bill indicting the trio. Julia Quander appeared later that month, in the case entitled the *Commonwealth vs. Julia Quander*, and pleaded not guilty to assault and trespass. She was convicted by a jury, fined five dollars, and held as committed until the fine and court costs were paid. The same day, in *Commonwealth vs. Felix Quander*, Felix also pleaded not guilty. A different jury of twelve men was convened to hear the evidence presented against him. The jury was unable to agree on a verdict and adjourned for the evening. The next morning, the jury continued their deliberations, whereupon Felix was promptly convicted, fined fourteen dollars, plus costs, and directed to be committed and held in jail until all assessments were paid in full.

Within a matter of weeks, Felix was in Fairfax County Courthouse again, this time filing a request that indictments that had been handed down against himself and Joseph Quander be dismissed. The petition was denied. A few days later, Felix and Joseph were again before the judge. This time, Felix was charged with assault with intent to kill, a felony offense as opposed to the August Court misdemeanor convictions. The court agreed to release Felix, who pleaded not guilty to the allegations, provided a five-hundred-dollar bond was posted to ensure that he would appear to answer the charges at the court's next term. Joseph Quander, as recorded in *Commonwealth vs. Joseph Quander*, was also indicted for the felony offense of assault. Like Felix, he entered a plea of not guilty and was released upon his own recognizance, provided he posted a one-hundred-dollar bond to ensure his appearance at court during the next term to answer the charges.[2] At this point, the records become sketchy, and the outcomes of the two cases are not apparent. But in the July term of 1869, almost a full year later, Joseph Quander reappears in the court record, asking to be released from jail on bail. Whether he simply was unable to post the one-hundred-dollar bail required the prior year or this is a new case cannot be determined. The court ordered Joseph's release but directed him to report back on August 1, 1869, to answer an indictment.[3]

That Felix and Julia had frequent scrapes with the state of Virginia cannot be doubted. It was readily apparent that it did not take much to set them off. In the fall of 1874, Felix and Julia were again in trouble, this time "for an assault upon an officer in discharge of his office." This time, Constable Charles Landstreet rode his horse to the Quander farm to take one of Felix's cows to satisfy nonpayment of taxes. When Felix showed Landstreet a claim of homestead exemption for the sought property, Landstreet evidently ignored him. Julia Quander then placed herself in the cow pen, blocking Landstreet's access with an axe in her hand. According to the court record, she "struck at the officer with the poll of it...the officer caught the axe and took it from her, at the same time drawing his pistol...Felix Quander had not said a word to his wife—had not directed her to put the axe down."

Landstreet left on foot, Mrs. Quander having chased away his horse. When he returned that evening with a posse, he was greeted at the cow pen with not only an axe but also with a pot of boiling water, a pile of stones, and a butcher knife in Julia's hand. The posse arrested Felix, who was brought before a magistrate and fined ten dollars. When asked why he did not admonish his wife during the incident, Felix explained it would have been of no use as she was deaf on cloudy days and could hear only a little on sunny days.[4]

Is it any wonder that Felix, Julia, and company would continue to get into all types of trouble? Still whenever I think about what the racial atmosphere must have been for such a strong-willed Black man, I feel great empathy for Felix. He appears to have had some exposure and appreciation for whatever life's offerings were for the free Black man of the mid to late nineteenth century. Being an integral part of the landowning Quander family of Fairfax County, which included his Uncle Osmond Quander who owned more than three hundred acres in 1850, Felix certainly must have had mixed feelings about who he was and the troubles he ran into seemingly at every turn. The burden of behaving himself must have been great. Perhaps Felix simply could not contain himself, whether in frustration or anger or conversely, because he was having too good a time to care. Either way, the end to his considerable troubles was far from in sight.

On March 21, 1879, the *Alexandria Gazette* published a series of resolutions adopted by the Society for the Prevention of Thievery, whose membership consisted primarily of a group of White Northern men who had settled in the Mount Vernon area of Virginia. The resolutions targeted Felix Quander, who in the sight of these men was no more than an old negro (small "n" intended) thief and trouble-maker. Believing he had been unjustly singled out, Felix, totally illiterate but buttressed by the assistance of a cadre of local supporters, issued a response letter published on March 24, 1879, in the same

Gazette and also the *Washington Republican*, the latter a newspaper in Washington, DC. He took strenuous issue with the society's allegations and resolutions, noting that the allegations were false and malicious and that he wished to present the "true version of the case." In a third-person literary style, Felix's letter described him as an old (he was about fifty-two) colored man who had raised a large family, who had always been free, and who had acquired a respectable fifteen acres of land some nineteen miles from the Washington, DC, markets. Further, it related how he or a family member hauled fruit, garden vegetables, and other products to the Washington markets several days per week.

Felix noted that five weeks earlier, about February 14, 1879, his wife Julia and one of his sons had traveled to Washington to market some chickens. When they arrived at about 8:00 a.m., a man named John Truax appeared. He lived in Woodlawn, Virginia, at least six miles from Felix's Mount Vernon Road home. Truax requested that a policeman arrest both Quanders for stealing Truax's chickens. The two were arrested and locked up in the station house. Taken before the Honorable Judge Snell, Truax was unable to make his case against them. Julia Quander and her son were freed but not before Truax was rebuked by the judge.

Truax decided to try his luck again by lodging the same complaint in Virginia. He swore out a second warrant for the exact same offense. John H. Sartin, a peace officer, was to execute the warrant. Sartin assembled what Felix's letter referred to as "an armed mob of eighteen ruffians" who—amid racist—yells, curses, threats, and cries of "lynch him!" called for the "nigger" to come out. Arriving at Felix's house about four o'clock on Sunday morning, February 16, 1879, they surrounded the house in which huddled Quander, his wife, two near-grown boys, three half-grown girls, one of whom was sick, and three small children. The Quanders' total armament consisted of one loaded musket without a cap (without which they could not return fire), one empty musket, and an old ax. When reinforcements arrived, raising the posse to thirty-three men, they attacked the house, shooting through the doors, windows, knotholes, and every crevice they could see in the increasing light of the new day. They shot until there were no windows left in the house, until all the doors had fallen from their hinges, and then set the house afire.

A February 16, 1879, diary entry by T. M. Blunt, one of the recruited posse members, reads as follows:

> Sunday, Feb. 16: Cool and Cloudy. I stop home and in the house till 1, and just as I was finishing my dinner, Constable C. H. Sartin calls, and presses me into service to help arrest Felix Quander and family. When we arrive there we find upwards of thirty people gathered to help to arrest them, and the Quanders were armed with guns, axes, picks and brickbats, and threatened to kill the first man that came in the house. After several hours of ineffective attempts to arrest them without violence, they were shot and secured.

Notice that Blunt's entry is at odds with Felix's letter concerning how the Quander family was armed and does not refer to the posse's middle-of-the-night disorderly actions and threats. Blunt seems to accept having thirty men overpower a single family as business as usual.

After the heavy shooting and because the house was so badly burned and damaged, the Quanders tried to surrender. However, coming out of the house, they were driven back by a hail of gunfire, which injured four of them. Not until about five o'clock that afternoon did this brave posse approach the burned-out home, where they found the family wounded, some seriously. After ransacking what was left of the house, they arrested the family, loaded them into wagons, and hauled them to Alexandria. Although one of the boys was said to be dying from a gunshot wound to his head, no medical treatment was sought.[5]

The following day, February 17, 1879, Justice Owen Kirby examined the warrant for the arrest of Joseph Quander and "July" Quander. Stating that he neither issued the warrant nor authorized it to be issued, Kirby found the manner in which the Quanders had been treated to be reprehensible and the manner in which the arrest had been executed to be intolerable, including shooting the Quander home to pieces. Truax's complaint, which was a different matter, was referred to Esquire Thomas Brown, who also found that Truax had failed to successfully sustain his chicken theft allegations.

But the matter was not at end, for new warrants alleging the family had resisted arrest were procured. The family was obliged to post bond and appear at the Fairfax County Court on March 17, 1879. They were released on their own recognizance, but in the interim, a grand jury of the Fairfax County Court issued a true bill against Felix, Julia, and Felix Jr. for the alleged assault against Constable John H. Sartin while he attempted to arrest them. The Quanders were directed to appear in court again in May 1879 for the offense of resisting arrest by Constable Sartin and the posse. For this offense, Felix Sr. was fined twenty dollars, and Felix Jr. was fined ten dollars; Julia was discharged without a fine. The writer of a *Gazette* article entitled "Last of the Quander Case" noted, "The Quanders, who bear a very bad reputation in Fairfax, are said to be descendants of the old Mt. Vernon slaves, thus showing a very great deterioration in that historic family."[6]

And thus drew to a close an intriguing chapter in the Quander family history.

But Felix was far from finished. Only a few months later, the August 1, 1879, *Alexandria Gazette* reported he had been arrested for assault the previous day when Constable James Watkins was sent to the Accotink neighborhood where Felix resided to arrest Felix for the January 1879 theft of a horse harness.

And so began another round of news articles. Although a few touted Felix's alleged virtues, the racist climate of the times, plus the community's low regard for Felix and his sector of the Quander family, generally resulted in a sound drubbing of the Quander name. On August 2, 1879, a follow-up article appeared in the *Gazette* that was reprinted on August 4 in the Washington, DC, *Evening Star*. The August 2 *Gazette* article noted that when Constable Watkins attempted to present the warrant, Felix refused to listen and cut the allegedly stolen harness into pieces. Felix was finally subdued by the posse Watkins had assembled but not before guns were fired. Felix appeared before Justice Kirby who found Felix guilty of stealing the harness and sentenced him to receive thirty-nine lashes. Felix evaded his guards, jumped through a window, and escaped to the District of Columbia where he told the assembled press the sad tale of his persecution. The unnamed writer concluded by noting that the complainant was a Northerner, a man from Pennsylvania, and that the many other Northerners living in the Accotink area all allegedly agreed that Felix Quander was a man with vicious propensities.

I assume this closing point was part of an attempt to isolate Felix from his neighbors who, being "Northerners," would presumably not be sympathetic with the Southern Cause. Reconstruction had not too long ended, and there were pockets of residents throughout the region whose racial and political attitudes were at variance with the attitudes of their close neighbors. The outcome of Felix's trial, regardless of the circumstances, highlighted the plight that Blacks faced in Fairfax County in 1879. In this atmosphere, securing a "fair trial" when accused by a White man of theft might have been an oxymoron.

Two days later, on August 4, 1879, the *Gazette* referred to the story Felix related to the press once he reached Washington, DC, as "a most heartrending tale of persecution and outrage, only fault of which is its utter want of truth." The same day, the *Evening Star* printed a letter to the editor attributed to "Felix Quander Sr., his 'x' mark." Although the true author of the letter remains a mystery, the person was obviously sympathetic to Felix's plight. He challenged the *Evening Star* to measure up to its assertions that the newspaper aspired to do justice to all persons without regard to race, color, or previous condition and to report the entire sequence of events regarding Felix in a fair, accurate manner. The long letter denied all the allegations reported in the *Gazette* and asserted that Felix could establish his innocence before any man who was not blinded by prejudice.[7]

It was only from this letter that readers could gain a sense of the unfolding events from Felix's perspective. All earlier news articles gave snatches of information generally from the perspective of the arresting official or the court. They never suggested that the alleged harness theft in January 1879 had renewed an ongoing problem between Kirby and Quander. In contrast, the August 4, 1879, letter took *Evening Star* readers back ten years to an accusation of horse theft. Felix's horse had gotten loose and wandered on to the property of Richard Roberts, a White man. Finding the horse quartered at Roberts's property, Felix retrieved the horse and took it home. Roberts swore out an arrest warrant against Quander. Owen Kirby, at that time a constable, was charged with executing the warrant. He assembled a large posse of armed men that converged upon Felix's house, shooting, cursing, and yelling racial epithets.

The letter related that when Felix sought to have a new trial before another judge, Kirby not only blocked the effort but also came to Quander's farm and threatened to take Felix's horse. A scuffle ensued, allegedly instigated by Kirby, and Felix was indicted for assaulting an officer and resisting arrest. Felix asserted that ever since that incident of 1869 or 1870, Kirby, now a magistrate, and his friends had pursued him, most recently concerning the false complaint of a stolen harness. Kirby's attitude about what was fair seems to have changed perhaps because he now found himself at the center of a dispute with Felix.

The letter noted that Kirby issued the warrant in connection with the stolen harness to Constable James Watkins, authorizing him to search Felix's premises and to arrest Felix and his son Joseph. At the trial, Kirby denied Felix's request to assemble witnesses who could attest to the true ownership of the harness. When they gathered anyway, Kirby refused to let them speak. In Felix's attributed words, "Kirby sentenced me 'to receive thirty-nine lashes, on [my] naked back, well laid on.'" Not one to submit peacefully, Felix added,

> I refused to be whipped, and run [sic].
> I was pursued by Kirby's friends, his quiet law
> abiding citizens all armed with guns and pistols,
> who opened fire upon me and shot it up until
> they had my legs, head and arms full of shot and
> bullets and exhausted their ammunition. When

they pressed me too close and my wind was falling, I was forced to turn and fight them back with stones, and when breathed pushed on. This occurred several times.

Felix concluded his letter by asserting that the posse that came to his house with guns on July 31, 1879, in support of Watkins's unsuccessful effort to arrest him on July 25, were part of the same mob of armed men who besieged his house all day on February 16, 1879, who shot his house to pieces, set fire to it, and also wounded five members of his family.

On the same day, August 4, 1879, that the letter to the editor appeared in the *Evening Star* over Felix's name, another damning article appeared in the *Alexandria Gazette*, which in its opening sentence referred to Quander as "the colored desperado of Fairfax County, Virginia, who is made such a martyr of by some of the radical press in Washington." Noting that even Northern men were willing to testify as to Felix's bad character, the *Gazette* asserted that the only persons who had interfered with Felix's lawlessness were law officers who were justified in everything they had done in arresting and punishing him. Further, the article asserted,

> It was exceedingly [illegible word] for the radicals to make a martyr of a "negro" in the South, but especially so now, when elections are approaching and when its martyrs produce a telling effect upon the susceptible voters of the North; but making one out of Quander is ridiculous to those who know him, among whom are many good and true republicans, who will volunteer to give evidence that would be sufficient to convict him even before a northern jury.[8]

On August 9, 1879, the *Gazette* took strenuous exception to an article that had appeared in the *Evening Star* the day before. The Virginia paper objected to the attention given by the Washington press to Quander, "the 'negro' thief and desperado of Fairfax county, [who] gets radical scribblers to write for him, with as much apparent willingness as though they were the emanation of an important personage." The *Gazette* continued, "Possibly if they were aware that Quander is held in the same estimation by his neighbors that notorious low colored criminals of Washington are held by theirs, they might not grant him so much of their space."

August 12, 1879, was a red-letter day for Felix. The *Gazette* published both an editorial and a major feature article about "the 'negro' thief and desperado." Once again, the editor railed against the radical press of Washington, Cincinnati, and points north, which had taken so much interest in the case. Noting that Felix had finally been arrested and was now safely secured in jail, the editor reminded his readers and the court that there was an outstanding punishment of thirty-nine lashes still to be administered upon Felix's naked back and that the public trusted the authorities to deliver the punishment as soon as Felix was recovered from the wounds he received incidental to his capture. In fact, the editor concluded,

> Fortunately for the reputation of the people of Fairfax county, who would otherwise be accused by the radical newspapers of cruel barbarity for their treatment of Quander, his neighbors, as heretofore stated, though northern men and sound republicans, voluntarily testify to his notoriously bad character and maliciously vicious disposition. He would not receive a lash too many if the penalty of his sentence were doubled.

Felix's arrest had not been accomplished peacefully. The police had received information he might attempt to return to Virginia from Washington, DC, via the Hunting Creek Bridge. Officers Bettis and Franks waited by the bridge until they were approached by a horse-drawn wagon driven by a woman whom they suspected was Julia Quander. The *Gazette* reported that Mrs. Quander gazed placidly at the two men, commenting that all she was doing was getting her groceries. Felix was not with her, but the officers noticed a man walking rapidly toward them. When the man spoke, Bettis recognized Felix's voice and seized him immediately. Felix broke loose and ran toward the creek, followed by the two officers who fired at him. Within minutes, he was cornered by a fence he could not climb and was arrested.

Interestingly, at this point in the story, the *Gazette* reporter shifted to Felix's perspective on the events leading to his capture. Felix told the reporter that he and Julia left Washington, DC, in a wagon in the late afternoon but were stopped in Alexandria by Thomas Hayes, who attempted to arrest him. Breaking free, Felix ran down Washington Street to the canal, where a crowd that had been in pursuit lost sight of him. He stopped to talk to a colored man in the street and related to him his troubles. When two officers came up and asked him if he was Quander, he ran off with them in hot pursuit, firing their guns. Felix related that he was shot in the calf of his right leg, but he continued to run, bleeding and in pain, until he was too exhausted to continue. The officers who overtook him subdued him with a billy club, cutting his head.

Felix's incarceration touched off another round of news articles, as the southern-minded, racially motivated *Gazette* apparently felt compelled to defend not only itself but also the actions taken against Felix by members of the local constabulary. The first of the new salvos was a *Gazette* editorial on August 13, 1879, which noted that the way in which the "radical newspapers" of the country wrote about Felix, using phrases such as "Southern Outrages," encouraged their readers to believe that Negroes were being cruelly used in the South. According to some of these papers, which were not named, "Quander is represented by them as an honest, intelligent, educated and highly respectable colored man, whose thrift and superiority to the degenerate F.F.V.'s [first families of Virginia] who are his neighbors have evoked the envy and malice of the latter, by whom he is persecuted in a way that would shame a Zulu."

Typical among those so-called radical papers was the *National Republican*, which ran an article on August 14, 1879, bearing the title, "Persecuting an Old Man—The True Facts in the Case of Felix Quander." The author, D. W. Glassie, signed his name as attorney for Quander. Glassie indicated that his job was to set forth the facts and let the community be the judge about Quander. He described Felix as a law-abiding man who had always had the confidence and respect of the White population. The remainder of Glassie's long article details the various charges erroneously brought against Felix, including horse, chicken, and harness theft, as well as assault and resisting arrest. Glassie also touches on how several of the Quanders were injured when the posse shot up and destroyed the Quander house.

Glassie points out that Kirby refused to recuse himself from presiding at the harness theft trial, refused to hear evidence from the defense, and—having found Quander guilty—declined to stay the punishment of thirty-nine lashes until an appeal was taken. At this, Felix ran off to avoid being whipped. "This, and only this," Glassie commented, "is the 'negro's' offense. For this he is driven from his home, and for this the forces of Alexandria are invoked, and poor old man Quander is shot to pieces." In his final paragraph, Glassie stated,

> Some of the better citizens of Alexandria assured me today that he was a good quiet citizen, much abused, and that they would defend him with their word and some means. The better class of citizens are not, as I learn, in sympathy with these outrages upon this old man... Quander is still in jail under the kind-hearted, humane jailer, B. R. Cline, who treats the old man more like a wounded brother than a vicious man...notwithstanding that Quander is severely wounded and battered, [Kirby] demanded his person that he might be whipped the 'thirty-nine lashes well laid on'; but the surgeon refused to let him be removed.

The reaction at the *Gazette* to the *National Republican* article was swift and specific. The next day, August 15, 1879, a letter to the editor signed by "One Who Knows" sharply criticized Glassie's effort to portray Quander as a saint and a martyr. Claiming to have known Felix for about twenty years, the *Gazette* writer asserted he was the opposite of the image Glassie sought to portray and that perhaps Glassie was taken in by Quander and his cohorts. He dismissed as preposterous claims that Felix was being bulldozed and that only evildoers need fear Justice Kirby and Constable Sartin. The anonymous acquaintance concluded by noting, "It is to be hoped that these attempts to force public opinion to the favor of a persistent violator of law will cease."

On August 21, 1879, approximately ten days after Felix was jailed, the *Gazette* ran an update under the title "Badly Wounded." The article said Quander was suffering from the gunshot wound to his left leg, which he received while attempting to escape. (When Felix first related this incident to the press, he said his right leg had been injured.) The leg is referred to as badly swollen and inflamed with doctors expressing concern that it might have to be amputated. And that is the end of the story. After this, Felix vanishes from the public record, and we know neither the date nor the cause of his death. Although he may have succumbed to blood loss and infection from the final gunshot wound, I like to think Felix survived a few more years as his irascible self to annoy the good citizens of Fairfax County.

CHAPTER 7

•⁺•⁺◆⁺◆⁺◆⁺•

Quander Place
A Washington, DC, Historic Site

The writer of Felix Quander's letter to the editor of the *Alexandria Gazette* on March 24, 1879, related how Felix or members of his family hauled fruit and garden vegetables from his fifteen-acre farm to the Washington, DC, markets several days per week, apparently ever since the Civil War. The city Felix would have seen immediately after the end of the war in April 1865 would have been quite different from the post-Reconstruction city of 1879. The streets and houses, as well as the racial makeup of the population, would have changed dramatically.

When Pierre L'Enfant laid out his plans for Washington, DC, he envisioned that the large yards behind the houses would provide tranquil places for the neighbors in the young national capital to visit, and indeed, this occurred when the city first took shape. Servants' quarters and carriage houses were generally constructed in the rear of the main houses, but even these buildings were maintained in good repair because they were an integral part of the property. During the war, this genteel existence was turned upside down when thousands of soldiers were quartered in the city, and vacant land for erecting barracks and camping places was at a premium. Paths that previously had seen only foot and carriage traffic suddenly began to look like miniature streets.

L'Enfant's plan, which was for a city of approximately one hundred thousand persons, was doomed at the end of the Civil War when thirty thousand to forty thousand newly freed African Americans poured into the capital under the mistaken belief that if they could only reach Washington, they would find protection and have their needs supplied by the federal government. As a pre-1920 study by Howard University sociology professor William H. Jones noted, the new arrivals knew nothing about city life. Most of these poor, needy, illiterate newcomers slept in tents or under trees, creating a menacing overpopulation problem and an extreme housing shortage. The quickest solution was to convert the deep backyards into income-producing residential sites, tuck ins behind and between what were far grander neighborhoods. Lots were cut in two, and the rear portions were sold and developed. An extensive system emerged in which the land and shacks on the interior alleys of the street blocks were owned independently of the lots and houses fronting the original streets.

Although many Southern cities attracted an influx of freed African Americans after the end of the war, the nation's capital attracted more than its share of such individuals, who quickly learned that life was hard here and that they were unwelcome. Vilified by the White residents, they were also not welcomed by the small but rapidly emerging Black middle class, many of whom were of mixed racial heritage. They, like their White neighbors, did not relish the perceived threatening presence of their ignorant, darker-skinned, "shiftless" brethren, who—without training or education—had no means of getting ahead.

As James Borchert noted in *Alley Life in Washington: Family, Community, Religion, and Folklife in the City, 1850–1970*, entire communities struggled in makeshift squalid housing in back alleys too frequently filled with vermin, violence, and frustration.[1] One of these undesirable sites was Quander Place (aka Quander Alley or Street), located in southeast Washington, adjacent to the historic Washington Navy Yard.[2] Occupying a portion of Square 743, Lot 23, Quander Place was bounded on the north by M Street, on the south by N Street, on the west by First Street, and on the east by New

Jersey Avenue.[3] A second alley, Van Street, was located on the rear portion of Lot 23, which was one of the original one-hundred-by-one-hundred-foot building lots in the area. The existence of the then unnamed alley is indicated on some early 1880s city maps, which reflect a small street cut with existing households in place.

The Square 743 Quander Place site was not just another alley where poor freed Blacks set up housekeeping in the post-Civil War decades. During the Battle of Washington in August 1814, as the War of 1812 drew to its indecisive conclusion, the Washington Navy Yard was peppered with cannon fire after British naval vessels penetrated our defenses and sailed into the Eastern Branch (the Anacostia River), just south of where Quander Place was later located. Troops disembarked from the ships, surrounded the Washington Navy Yard, and burned it to the ground, leaving in their wake ruined timbers, cannon, and other evidence of the U.S. naval military presence.[4] The Quander-Van site was the location for the quartering of British troops as they took up temporary residence in the nation's capital.

The archaeological significance of the Quander site was noted in a survey associated with the planned expansion of Building 213 in the Navy Yard Annex: "The archaeological resources at the Quander Alley site are significant primarily because they can provide information about the quality of life that existed in an urban alley environment in the District of Columbia during the later nineteenth and early twentieth centuries. Historical information indicates that the deposits on the site are reflective of black, working class households."[5]

The City Directories and federal censuses of 1900 and 1910 show the residents of Quander Place were Black, with typical occupations as domestics, porters, and unskilled general laborers, with an occasional carpenter or store proprietor. The 1900 U.S. Census shows a distinct pattern of racial segregation within Square 743, with the Black residents confined primarily to the internal alleys. Eighty-six of the ninety-two dwellings located on the facing streets (M, N, New Jersey, and First) were occupied by White families while fifty-one of the fifty-three dwellings located on Quander Place and Van Street were occupied by Blacks. This segregation was not unique to Quander Place, as working class Blacks were caught in this pattern throughout much of Washington during the late nineteenth and early twentieth centuries. Borchert estimated that in 1890, approximately thirty thousand people, representing about forty percent of the city's African American population, lived in alleys of this type.[6] Because the city was subjected to intense land use and workers needed to be able to walk to work, Black households frequently crowded into the alleys close to the work sites.

The Quander site archaeological evaluation for the proposed demolition to Building 213 involved digging several trenches by backhoe, and several three-by-three-foot sections were hand excavated in and about the abandoned wells and privies. Retrieved from among the pebbles and cinders were combs, bottles, ceramic items, buttons, dolls, pipes, and other items of daily use, often fragmented but occasionally in one piece. Excavated food remains such as bone fragments from cows, pigs, sheep, chickens, and turkeys; fruit pits; shells from oysters, mussels, and clams; and fish vertebrae revealed the types of foods the Quander Place residents ate, and charred materials, when analyzed, indicated what vegetables were consumed.

In 1990, archaeologists Charles D. Cheek and Amy Friedlander published "Pottery and Pig's Feet: Space, Ethnicity, and Neighborhood in Washington, DC, 1880–1940."[7] Using excavations from Quander Place and adjacent N Street homes, the authors examined various components of alley and street life. Both deposit areas consisted of compacted sheets of materials, including trash excavated from trash pits that had been dug in the rear yards or outhouses turned into trash pits when a family obtained indoor plumbing. Their broad conclusions were predictable. Whites had more diversity in their ceramic ware, although its quality was largely the same as Blacks' ceramic ware. The Whites had significantly better glassware, probably indicative of the consumption of wines and higher-priced beverages. Both groups ate chicken, beef, pork, and fish, but Whites had more expensive cuts of meat, generally cut by clean-cutting equipment, while the Blacks' butchers used saws and more crude cutting instruments. The Black residents also left a high residue of bones from pig feet and opossum, as well as mustard greens, watermelon seeds, and pecan shells. All these foods showed a strong carryover from the Southern, rural history of Quander Place occupants, virtually none of whom were listed in U.S. Federal census records as having been born in Washington, DC.

The article extended earlier work, particularly Borchert and the *Eligibility Report*. The authors supported Borchert's thesis that early twentieth-century social reformers' emphasis upon squalor and deviant behavior in alley households failed to recognize that this alleged deviant behavior was the product of different cultural attitudes that derived from the adaptation of Black rural migrants to the constraints of urban poverty.[8] Quander Place provided an urban microcosm of life at the poorer end of the working class community. The results of the archaeological digs conducted at the Quander site on Lot 23 represented the material remains of a widespread feature of the urban landscape rather than an isolated phenomenon. The races lived within close proximity, usually separated only by a backyard fence, without being truly integrated. But was alley life a pocket of crime, disease, social disorganization, and pathology, as some studies have concluded, or was this life one of tightly knit communities that provided a sense of identity and belonging as other analyses have maintained?[9]

Early twentieth-century opinion held that alley life was, at best, sordid and unwholesome. An undated, pre-1920 article in the *Evening Star* titled "Squalid Alleys Encourage Crime" noted "that underworld characters have found refuge in sordid hovels in the capital city, and that inhabitation in alleys has taken on a character of its own which, despite efforts to reform both the alleys and their inhabitants, does not seem to be meeting with success."

That the conditions were nothing short of squalid is clearly indicted in Charles Frederick Weller's *Neglected Neighbors*, a series of stories of early twentieth-century life in the alleys, tenements, and shanties of Washington, DC.[10] Weller was a well-respected housing authority of his day, having chaired several benevolent efforts to improve the quality of housing nationwide. Although Weller's contemporary opinion was that the alleys provided an incubator for laziness and vice and were dens of squalor and disorganization, he was nonetheless sympathetic to residents trapped in alley life. In *Neglected*

Neighbors, he wrote about Clarence, a sick child who lived with his family in Van Street, the alley immediately parallel to Quander Place. Weller noted that Clarence and his family's story of extreme human suffering and deterioration in Van Street might well be told about the many shacks and shanties that existed throughout Washington, DC, at the time. In the story, Clarence survives, but many outcomes might be worse, Weller argued, because the future was being neglected and no members of the degraded households were being rescued from the ill effects of unwholesome alley life.

The facts upon which *Neglected Neighbors* was based were included in a 1906 report that was sent to every U.S. congressman and selected influential citizens and newspapers around the country. Congress finally acted on May 1, 1906, and mandated that these properties either be condemned and closed or that compulsory repairs of these dwellings, which were unfit for human habitation, be made and maintained.

How the site obtained the name "Quander" remains uncertain, although City Directories from the early 1890s show a Julia Quander, a grocer and laundress, lived at 109 Quander Place and at times other relatives—Frank Quander and Harry Quander—lived there as well.[11] During my research, I was fortunate to locate two sisters, former residents of 158 Quander Place.[12] One of the sisters, Betty Douglas Anderson (b. 1920), volunteered that as a child, she was told that the Quanders were the first family of any prominence to live in the block and simply named the street after themselves. There may have been some truth to this claim, as 109 Quander was the only brick house in the block at the time (c. 1890–1943). The other sister, Helen Douglas Hawkins (b. 1918), lived at 158 Quander Place between 1932 and 1942. She recalled both Julia and Harry Quander, although she did not know whether they were husband and wife or siblings. She remembered the Quanders seemed to have an interest in more than one house on the block. Absentee White landlords owned several of the houses. Mrs. Hawkins speculated that Mrs. Quander collected rent for them or leased houses for subletting to the many renting families in the block. Julia Quander seems to have had an entrepreneurial spirit because everyone in the neighborhood knew she used to operate a store from her home before the 1930s.

Mrs. Hawkins recalled that Quander Place was so run-down that it should have been demolished years previously, as the history of municipal neglect and poor living conditions in the city alley dwellings was legendary. Still there was a sense of community, a sense of quiet dignity in Quander Place, and for that, she would always be grateful.

The dwellings on Square 743, Lot 23, like those of the neighboring alley lots, continued to be occupied primarily by the Black working class until 1942 when the area was razed to allow World War II era expansion of the Navy Yard. When Quander Place was finally closed in 1943 and the U.S. Navy tore down all the housing to expand the Navy Yard for the war effort, it was not a moment too soon, as the character of the area had changed significantly as more people flowed into Washington to support the war effort. Living in such squalid locations as Quander Place had become less and less desirable, a situation that would inevitably have led to more neglect and an increase in crime.

It would have been reasonable to assume in 1943 that we had heard the last of Quander Place. But from then until the last few years of the twentieth century, the U.S. Navy devoted Square 743 to cartography and the study of military needs connected to topography. However, as technology advanced, the need for a separate topographical site declined. Federal and DC government planners realized that the time had come to redevelop the entire area and replace the cement plants, trash transfer stations, and run-down housing. Among the sites available for redevelopment was part of Lot 23 in Square 743, which had included Quander and Van Streets before they were absorbed into the Navy Yard during the 1943 expansion. The entire area was razed to make way for modernization.

When I learned that redevelopment was going to occur throughout the area, I contacted Sharon Ambrose then the DC councilmember for Ward Six. I was directed to prepare a presentation, the essence of which set forth the historical significance of the Quander family in American history and requested that Quander Street be restored in its previous location. In response to Councilmember Ambrose's request that Quander Street be restored as an integral component of the site redevelopment, the developer stated they appreciated the historical significance and sustained collective contributions of the Quander family and would place a historical market at the entrance of the restored street. A later development company advised me that they intended to exploit the historical importance of the Battle of Washington at this site during the War of 1812 as well as the long-time presence of the Quander family, one of America's oldest Black families. Quander Street may be only two blocks long, but it is rich in history!

Quander Street at First Street and New
Jersey Avenue, S.E., Washington, DC

CHAPTER 8

+ + + + + +

The Quander Family Reunion
and Quanders United

I used to think that family reunions were largely restricted to African Americans who wished to pull their extended families back together to reminiscence about "the good ol' days." I knew many Southern Blacks had migrated North or to the largest nearby city, creating situations in which parents and siblings were seen less frequently, and extended family often not at all, unless a structured event was planned. The family reunion served as a rallying place for family to share their love, lives, and experiences, to seek solace and strength to carry on, and perhaps to show off how well they were doing.

Now in my older years, what I initially surmised about the family reunion as a "black thing" is still largely true, except that the celebration has spread like "topsy" and is no longer primarily an African American event. It has become part of American culture as more and more White Americans hold their own reunions as they seek to stem the same negative effects that the dissolution of the family and long-distance relationships has created. Still in my estimation, the more intimate, down-home gathering remains largely a black thing, an event that grew out of the post-slavery era when closely knit family members or fellow former slaves who were like family decided to maintain ties across the miles. A typical example is the Somerset Homecoming, an expanded reunion of the slave descendants of those who worked on the Somerset Plantation in North Carolina. Organized by Dorothy Spruill Redford in 1989, the homecoming gathered people from across the nation to pay tribute to their ancestors.

Long before the Somerset Homecoming, the desire to keep the family together manifested itself in 1869 with the creation of the Still Family Reunion in Virginia. That reunion has continued to the present. I doubt any of the Still reunion founders thought their efforts would be recognized over 150 years later as an outstanding example of a family seeking to know itself across many generations. But that is exactly what happened. Our newer family event, the Quander Family Reunion (QFR), was conceived for all the same purposes. Its founders, like the founders of the Still Family Reunion, never dreamed they were making history. But the story of the bumpy road the Quanders traveled to gain national and international recognition has more twists and turns than Felix Quander's tale and even more media coverage. It is a story of hurt feelings, jealousies, rival reunions, and interstate feuding. It is also a story of joy, insights, growth, and tremendous satisfaction and pride. In short, the history of the QFR is both a triumph and a cautionary tale.

Death is a sharp reminder of loss and passing time, and it was the deaths of James A. and Alcinda Lear Quander in 1925 that sparked the idea of a family reunion. Family members lamented that many of them had moved out of Fairfax County, Virginia, and mainly visited at funerals. Several Quander women, looking for domestic work, had relocated north of the Mason-Dixon Line around 1900 where some of them met their future husbands. Other family members had followed. Recognizing that they felt increasingly disconnected, a cadre of family decided to take action, and the annual QFR began to take shape.

Alcinda Lear Quander was the mulatto great-granddaughter of Tobias Lear, George Washington's personal secretary. Her husband James had a similarly long lineage, being the great-grandson of Nancy Carter and Charles Quander. James and Alcinda's oldest child, Emma, and Emma's husband, Thomas Harris—another mulatto descendant of Tobias Lear—hosted the first reunion on August 15,

1926, at their twenty-acre farm home in Woodlawn, Virginia. From this inconspicuous beginning, the QFR grew to be a recognized national institution. There were no library resources on reunions in those days; no computer, Internet, or web pages were available to help plan a family reunion. There was no *Reunions* magazine laying forth a master plan, suggesting events or offering tips on staging a successful family reunion. Planning, which took almost a year, took place around the dining room tables of Emma, in Virginia, and her sister Rose, in Berwyn, Pennsylvania. Their planning was all original work, executed using the mail (many family members lacked telephones), word of mouth, and mother wit.

What was the first QFR like? Several years before his death, I interviewed Lewis Lear Quander (1919–2003) who had vivid recollections of attending the 1926 reunion when he was seven years old. The reunion was a one-day event, but guests started to assemble the day before. There were no hotels for the colored to stay in, and besides, no one had money for such a luxury, so everyone just doubled and tripled up, creating a cozy but hot situation.

One of Lewis's many recollections of the first QFR remained dear to him. The children were playing in the expansive yard while the women were mainly in the kitchen and dining room preparing the meal. When dinner was served, with tables set up in the large country home dining room and screened-in back porch, most of the men were nowhere to be seen. Everyone, even the children, knew that Tom Harris, the host of the affair, was a drinker. He drank despite the fact that alcohol was illegal during Prohibition and condemned by his church at all times.[1] Most of the other men, being good Baptists and Methodists, were also supposed to abstain. Tom had made a batch of corn whiskey for the QFR and put it in a tub on ice by the woodshed behind the house. After sampling Tom's whiskey, at least half the men were more than tipsy to downright drunk. Some were immobilized on their backs in the tall grass behind the woodshed.

Susannah, Lewis's great aunt, came looking for the men to announce that dinner was ready. Hearing they may be in the shed, she headed in that direction, accompanied by some of the children.

What she saw horrified her: thoroughly inebriated men lying inert in the grass and others, also drunk, in the shed. Shocked and disgusted, she blurted out, "God help these drunken niggers!"

Lewis said, "Four or five of them were so drunk, they couldn't even stand up. Aunt Susannah was so mad she could have bitten a rattlesnake. The kids were all playing close by, not far from the woodshed. Our presence made the women even angrier since the children were eyewitnesses to this entire drunken and depraved incident. Some of my aunts and female cousins even pulled their husbands by their ears or collars, muttering under their breath things like, 'What a fool you've made of yourself!' and, 'You'd better eat this dinner, drunk or not.'"

Within a flash, the entire reunion knew all about it. The men had no choice but to drag themselves and each other to the tables to put some food with the liquor they had been consuming on empty stomachs. The weather was blazing hot, which made the situation even worse. The minutes of that first reunion politely omit this incident, noting only that forty-two people enjoyed "plenty of fried chicken and everything that goes with it." Lewis's recollections confirm that the menu was simple but good: fried chicken, succotash, mashed potatoes with gravy, and homemade ice cream. After the big dinner—and presumably after the men had sobered up—a brief business meeting was held, photographs were taken, and a short program was presented that included brothers Frank and George Wilson playing the guitar and singing a few numbers. And the first QFR came to an end.

Although the minutes indicate a prim and proper reunion, my research and conversations with Lewis have painted a vastly different, more personal picture of that event, one that demonstrates that the first reunion was a smashing success in many ways, achieving its stated objective of allowing family members to interact on all levels. They certainly did! Fittingly, at the business meeting, a motion was passed to adopt "Stick together" as the QFR motto.

The Quanders who attended the first four QFRs all hailed from Virginia and Pennsylvania. Most of them not only considered themselves distinct from the Maryland—Washington, DC, branch of the family (of which I am a member), but also they vehemently denied any relation and wanted nothing to do with us. For the first few years being descended from the original QFR founding group also served to exclude those Virginia Quanders who were not connected in some way to Mount Vernon. Most of the founders' common ancestors were Mount Vernon descended on both the White and Black sides of the family. Tobias Lear was known within the family as a White Quander ancestor. West Ford, a famously recorded Washington family slave and another known Quander ancestor, was born of a slave named "Venus and an unknown father." Despite Ford's uncertain paternity, it was widely believed he had Washington blood in his veins. The historical connection to George Washington and other national figures identified with the plantation was an element the QFR founding group jealously guarded. They believed they had a unique legacy that had to be protected and kept undiluted, and they drew a tight circle around themselves to the exclusion of many others who did not understand why they thought and acted as they did.

After much wrangling, at the fifth QFR in 1930, the "other" Virginia Quanders were superficially accepted. They were invited for dessert only—after the blessing, after the meal, and after the business meeting. It was a bitter pill. The hard feelings generated from these initial exclusions took years to smooth over. Gladys Quander Tancil recalled how her father fussed, "Aren't we all Quanders, descended from a common root? And here they are celebrating their Quanderness and holding a so-called Quander family reunion but excluding a large part of the Quander family. It's just not right!"

The second QFR was held at the home of Samuel and Rose Q. Harmon in Berwyn. Lewis, then eight years old, recalled being hot, anxious, and excited in the car on the long trip to Pennsylvania. The roads were poor, often dusty, and the pace seemed inordinately slow. Lewis's recollections were again lively and helpful, and the most detailed of those recollections revolved around another memorable, although sober, scene. Rose had a reputation for being unreasonably frugal. Lewis's word was *stingy*. Her meat menu consisted of an inadequate amount of extremely tough stewed chicken. The meat quickly ran out, and Emma, older sister and family tyrant, lit into Rose in front of everyone. Emma dressed Rose down about stretching the meal with a few tough old chickens and a lot of gravy. Although there was plenty of other food to eat, Emma's scene was the highlight of the day. Nonetheless, the well-mannered minutes of the second QFR note that "fifty-two Quander and Quander descendants [partook] of a bountiful dinner."

The minutes may have been different had Emma written them, but Rose served as secretary from 1926 until 1957. She kept the annual QFR minutes in a beautifully handwritten notebook that decades later would be the center of fractious arguments over its rightful ownership. Although scrupulously maintained, her minutes rarely reflect any disagreements, much less scenes of inebriation and loud, angry reprimands. Not much can be gleaned from Rose's censored descriptions about how the family was functioning. Her long tenure as secretary meant thirty-one years of sanitized records. Twenty years after her retirement as QFR secretary, her tradition was continued in *Fifty Golden Years: Minutes of Quander Family Reunion, 1926–1976*. This family publication painted an idyllic picture, avoiding any serious discussion on issues about which family members likely disagreed or argued.

Early on, probably in 1927 or 1928, the children became a standard part of the QFR program. Through the years, cousins recited poetry, sang and played music, and offered prayers and biblical readings. It was at the third QFR in 1928, in Woodlawn, Virginia, that the family first sang "Blessed Be the Tie That Binds," which has been sung at every QFR since then. Sixty-five family members of all ages were present at that reunion. At the business meeting, they decided the QFR should meet every other year in Virginia and Pennsylvania, and it has been so almost ever since.

The years flew past, with reunions held without fail. During the Great Depression, the Quanders traveled up and down the 1930s highway system on bumpy and dusty roads with multiple traffic lights, often through racially segregated small towns. They endured for hours to get to the reunions, often unable to stop at a restaurant or to use a rest room solely because of the color of their skin. Some family members traveled by train or bus, but the automobile was the transportation mode of choice. A car was not only the most convenient way to travel, but also it represented the most visible status symbol. Most family members drove less expensive vehicles like Fords and Chevrolets, but a few used the QFR to showcase their latest automotive acquisition, perhaps a Cadillac, Chrysler, Lincoln, or even a Packard. For some, the reunion was an event to show off new clothes or a smart new hat. Your possessions at the annual gathering served to deliver a positive message to parents, siblings, and the extended family to the effect of, "Hey, I ain't doing too bad, no matter what else you might have heard!"

1938 photo of four of the original 1926 founders of
the Quander family reunion, held on August 15, 1926,
at Woodlawn, Fairfax County, Virginia

The QFR slowly became less exclusive and allowed new locations and new members. In 1938, the thirteenth QFR, for example, was held at a home that was not owned by one of the founding members. But as if to remind everyone of the founders' Mount Vernon connections, the minutes noted that the reunion's location was "not very far from Mt. Vernon, called the home of our first president of the United States of America." After "eighty-four persons had eaten, until they couldn't eat any more, we went across the field to the home of Mr. and Mrs. James Quander [Gladys's parents] where the meeting and program were rendered." The minutes also noted that twenty-seven new members of the Quander family were added to the rolls.

With World War II came gasoline rationing, and although the family continued to hold local reunions, the interstate Virginia-Pennsylvania reunions had to be suspended. The Virginia Quanders used the time to reflect and keep track of who was away at war and how they were doing. Their reunions during World War II included a prayer vigil for the Quander men and women who were serving our country in places that many of the family members had never heard of. At the 1944 reunion, Vernon Butler spoke on what we, as Americans, were fighting for and particularly what the Negro was fighting for and hoped to receive as a result of our patriotic participation in defense of our nation. Butler's main thought was that as a result of the anticipated successful outcome of the war and despite the frustrations our race experienced from supporting the nation from the time of the Declaration of Independence to the present, this time, things should be different. Butler concluded that although there is still much that needs to be done with regard to fair treatment of the Negro, this is a different era, and attitudes are changing. The twentieth annual QFR was held on August 19, 1945, which, by coincidence, was the National Day of Thanksgiving declared by President Harry Truman. No member of the QFR had died in the war, despite the significant number who had seen combat, although James Simmons Jr., a Maryland Quander, died on D Day, June 6, 1944, during the Allied invasion of Normandy.

In 1947, the QFR returned to its traditional even year in Virginia and odd year in Pennsylvania schedule. From then until 1968, the QFR remained a regular event with attendance generally at sixty-five to seventy-five people in Pennsylvania and between eighty-five and one hundred in Virginia. The membership list constituted at least two hundred people.

By the 1960s, the QFR, after a thirty-five-year run, was drifting on automatic pilot, facing a collapse due to the deaths of the founders and other pillars of the QFR who had stepped up to take their place. There had been no permanent president for several years. Many of the younger people did not know each other, and the families were still expanding and more spread out than ever before. Too many of the youth had no knowledge of and, in some cases, little interest in their family's distinguished history. Although it seemed that the main purpose of the annual QFR was for living family to get together and celebrate each other's company, nevertheless, there was a consensus, at least among the older members, that family history was important. It was the glue that held everyone together. But what to do?

Help came in the form of Rev. Howard Wilson, who served as temporary president from 1963 to 1965. Under his tenure, the reunion was reinvigorated. At the thirty-ninth QFR in 1964, for the first time, a comprehensive set of QFR annual minutes from 1926 through 1963 was distributed. Beginning with the fortieth reunion in August 1965, a Saturday picnic and a Sunday community worship service were added to the prior Sunday-only format. Although prayer had always been an integral part of the reunions, the formal scheduling of a joint worship service was new. Older traditions, such as recognitions for the longest-married couple in attendance and the oldest person in attendance, were revived; and new ones, such as awarding a prize to the family or family members who had traveled the greatest distance to be present, were established. In fact, anyone who had achieved a milestone in their lives in the past year was recognized and honored.

In 1968, when I was a student at the Howard University School of Law, I attended my first QFR. Over the years, my father, James W. Quander (1918–2004), had casually known both Gladys Q. Tancil and Roberta H. Quander, first cousins and daughters of brothers James Henry and Robert Howard Quander respectively. Roberta invited my parents and me to come to the forty-third QFR. My dad knew about the QFR, but he had never been invited. I had never even heard of the event and had no concept of the breadth of our family's notable history. Arriving at the reunion was also my first visit to Quander Road. Imagine my delight at going to a street that had my name on it and then to the Quander Road Elementary School where the afternoon activities were conducted! Gladys told me that around 1900, the yet unnamed Quander Road was little more than a muddy wagon path. As more vehicles appeared, the path was widened and tarred. When Fairfax County officials needed a name for the street, they asked Gladys's grandfather, Charles Henry Quander, a successful dairy farmer and former slave whose acreage stretched along the road, what they should call it. He said, "Just call it Quander Road."

I met so many Quanders at that reunion I could not keep them straight. It was an unqualified pleasure to learn there was a whole other family about whom I knew nothing. Later, I asked my father why we did not know these people. He was unable to give a satisfactory answer, muttering something about a rumor of a family disagreement years ago between a Virginia Quander and a Maryland Quander that drove a wedge between the groups. Although having a few Maryland-DC Quanders in attendance was a significant departure from the QFR's standard practice of excluding "other" Quanders, the backroom chatter was not as inclusive as my parents and I would have been hoped. We were treated politely but like outside guests, not Quander relatives. The belief among the Virginia-based Quanders was that the exact connection between the two branches of Quanders was not firmly established. The QFR organizers did not extend an invitation for future reunions. The "unwelcome mat" was laid out, and it remained in active use for years. The beginning of the thaw came in 1984 when the Maryland-DC Quanders, whose legacy is older by decades than their Virginia counterparts, announced the planning of the Quander Tricentennial Celebration, 1684–1984, in which we would observe three hundred documented years in America. But I am getting ahead of the story.

I left the 1968 QFR with a thirst for knowledge. I began asking myself questions. Who was I? Where did I come from? Who were my forebears? Although I did not understand it at the time, I had been bitten hard by the genealogy bug. I was eager to learn family history, and I quickly developed the desire to share that knowledge now over a fifty-year quest. When I asked my dad why the Maryland-DC Quanders had not been holding family reunions over the years, he explained that our gatherings were of a different type, universally tied to Catholic Church events and communities, both in Upper Marlboro, Maryland, where his father John Edward Quander

(1883–1950) was from, and in Washington, DC. My dad told me that unlike our Virginia cousins, our group of Quanders shaped their legacy by building several church communities, both the congregations and the buildings themselves. Church archival records from as early as the 1840s at St. Mary of the Assumption Catholic Church in Upper Marlboro, for example, document regular Quander baptisms, confirmations, marriages, and funerals. These ancestors not only attended church, but also they laid bricks, cut boards, and prepared food for the work crews as they labored to build Black churches and found church-related associations. The latter included the founding of both the St. Mary's Beneficial Society and the Knights of St. John Commandery #74, both of which had a strong and lasting Quander presence. Organized in 1880, just fifteen years after the abolition of slavery, the Beneficial was created to address the many needs of African Americans in the parish. No public assistance was available at the time, and education and literacy were pressing requirements. One of the official founders of the Beneficial was John Henry Quander (c. 1830–c. 1896), my great-great-grandfather, who was born enslaved to Mordecai Plummer of Prince George's County.

In 1887, the Beneficial, in response to the routine racial discrimination and limitations imposed by St. Mary's White members, purchased a tract of land across from the church. By 1892, they had erected their own structure for meetings and to enjoy racial harmony and quietude. But there was still a thirst to do significantly more, and they determined to expand into a more Catholic doctrinal focus dedicated to Christian principles and civic virtue to supplement what they were already doing to help their fellow parishioners. They chose the Knights of St. John, founded in the year 1113, because it accepted colored members, although their affiliation was relegated to segregated commanderies. May 1889 saw the creation of the Knights of St. Mary's Association, Commandery No. 74, of the Knights of St. John. Gabriel Quander, my great-grandfather and son of John Henry Quander, is listed on the charter as one of the original nine members to whom the authority to create Commandery No. 74 was granted. As I learned of the extensive Quander involvement in these church-related endeavors, I understood my dad's explanation that these activities were similar to family reunions in that they kept the Maryland Quander family together. Like the QFR founders, these Quanders never thought their actions would, 150 years later, be viewed in the context of history.

My father was busy completing the final phase of his preparation for ordination as a permanent deacon in the Roman Catholic Church and was working full time, yet he yearned for wider communication among family members. When he retired from the federal government in 1974, he suggested to a cross section of Maryland-DC Quanders that we plan our own intergenerational Quander reunion. After much thought and discussion with many cousins, "Quanders United" was born. Although we would not officially adopt that name for several years, everyone agreed we needed a structure and that a family reunion should be planned. In October 1974, Dad issued a letter to the family announcing the new reunion and asking for information on the family's history. Because the mailing list was incomplete, word of mouth was critically important. We each designated ourselves as a committee of one to solicit everyone to attend.

The fledgling organization was far from the formal structure that would later emerge. We lacked the longevity of the QFR, and at the time, we were unaware of the internal problems that the QFR members were facing as their reunion aged. Quanders United decided to ignore the Virginia-Pennsylvania Quanders for the time being and concentrate upon our own reunion, the first ever to be held by the Maryland-DC Quanders. It was not a church event, although the planners assumed that a religious component, an opportunity to give thanks to the Almighty for the bountiful blessings that had been bestowed upon us all, would be an integral part of the first Quanders United reunion. Within a few months, on December 28, 1974, the big day arrived. All fears of an unsuccessful reunion were laid to rest when approximately 150 family members assembled at the Shrine of the Sacred Heart Church in Washington, DC, for the initiating mass. Following the mass, there was a bountiful gathering in the Gavin Center parish hall with a typical Quander menu reminiscent of the first 1926 QFR, "with plenty of fried chicken and everything that goes with it."

There was simply no containing the joy and excitement we each felt at having our first event, a chance for the oldest family members, all well past seventy years of age, to be officially presented to the family and a chance for everyone from the two primary Maryland branches, one from Upper Marlboro and the other from the Cheltenham-Rosaryville area, to meet and celebrate our reunion. Both communities are located in Prince George's County, Maryland. Time has blurred those distinctions and the even more historical fact that the ancestors initially all came from Charles County, Maryland, immediately to the south of Prince George's County.

Many of us did not know one another before that day. The crowning achievements of this first Quanders United reunion were creating a whole new web of relationships and bringing the Maryland-DC Quanders to come to know what "to be a Quander" really meant. The reunion was so well received that the spirit of being a Quander carried us well into the next year. We still had no formal structure, not even a name, but the second Quanders United reunion was even larger than the first one. In spite of our enthusiasm and strong turnout, the Maryland-DC reunion was not yet perceived as a threat to the QFR, although by 1975, some of the Virginia-based QFR Quanders were curious about what was going on in Washington, DC.

The following year, at the third Maryland-DC reunion, I delivered my first comprehensive family history presentation and was encouraged and gratified by the response. The presentation included a display of family photographs. My memories of this presentation are not of the family research I accomplished but the reluctance of several family members to part with their photographs, even if only for a day. After much coaxing and cajoling, I secured a large cross section of photos, most of which predated 1920 and many of which were taken prior to 1900. I had never seen most of the photographs, and not yet having developed a good sense of where their subjects fit into the family tree, accurately identifying everyone was a daunting task.

My wife Carmen, an internationally renowned artist, has a strong artistic sense of how to mount exhibits of all types. She undertook the job of carefully printing everyone's names on the photographs and mounting them on foam boards for display. The job took hours. Aided by my mother Joherra, Carmen stayed up the entire night before the third reunion to get the display correct. Her finished work was magnificent. The black-and-white photographs were generally in excellent condition, and Carmen's skill in presenting them rendered the result a work of art. When the family saw the exhibit, "oohs!" and "ahs!" were heard everywhere as people clustered around and recalled the people pictured. "There's Aunt Emma Hawkins!" someone would say. "She was married to Jeremiah Hawkins, the first mayor of North Brentwood, elected in 1924." And, "That's Uncle Mercer in his World War I Navy uniform. That photograph appeared on the front page of the *Afro* in 1919." And, "There's Dr. John Thomas Quander. He graduated from Howard University School of Medicine in 1909 but died of TB the following year."

And then there was Cousin Magdelene Gordon Nixon. Seeing the exhibit and not for a moment reflecting on its beauty and its message and all the work that went into it, she lit into Carmen. "That's not cousin so-and-so there. That's him over there!" she shrieked. "You have these two pictures reversed!" Carmen quickly corrected the mistake, trying her best to laugh it off. In retrospect, Cousin Magdalene's indignation was only a momentary source of discomfort, and her angry outburst underscored the importance of telling the family story accurately at all times, a key reason why I have penned this history. It wasn't funny at the time, but Cousin Magdalene's contribution to the reunion is recalled fondly forty years later. Like Emma ripping into Rose over the tough, stringy chicken, it's the type of event of which family reunions are made. How dull it would be if everything went off like clockwork, nothing went wrong, and the unexpected did not occur!

Although it took better than twenty years for the QFR to be considered an established institution, the offshoot new kid, Quanders United, matured at lightning speed. Blessed by the knowledge of what the Virginia-Pennsylvania cousins had done, 1977 found the Maryland-DC relatives hitting their stride. Enthusiasm remained high, and planning a fourth reunion was relatively easy. Many of the older family members were retired, and their children, my generation, also had time to devote to the effort. We reached out to the members of the QFR, and many of them responded favorably. Unfortunately, their participation belied the strife that lay ahead, but it demonstrated to all of us that cooperation was possible even if we were unable to point out the exact familial connections between our various family lines.

The fourth Quanders United reunion was the best yet. Although most of us were Catholic, we appreciated that other Christian faiths and even non-Christian religious traditions were also an integral part of our heritage. The planning committee decided that a change of venue was appropriate, and the event was held at the historic Nineteenth Street Baptist Church in Washington, DC. The service, which featured seven clerics, was ecumenical. We gathered in the beautiful sanctuary in the early afternoon on Saturday, December 10, 1977, with about 110 in attendance.

We were especially pleased to have James Walker, a research genealogist from the National Archives, speak to us about research-ing our roots. He stressed the importance of not delaying the search, noting that already too many living resources have died, leaving us with not one written word of family history. I knew this to be true. Although I had been fortunate to interview many of the most knowledgeable elder family members before they passed on, some died shortly before I could get to them. Walker's appearance at our family reunion was a major coup as he was in great demand both locally and nationally. The previous year, Alex Haley's book, *Roots*, was on the best-seller list, and the multi-night TV program of the same name had fascinated Americans, Black and White, throughout 1977. Suddenly, people everywhere wanted to know how to search for their historical and genealogical roots.

In contrast, the Quanders had established their basic and, in many cases, detailed roots decades before. Now we were in a clar-ification and verification stage rather than a start-up phase like so many other Americans. I had been researching the family's history since 1968 and had talked to many of the older Maryland-DC family members. In most cases, their individual knowledge was limited, but by piecing their stories together, I created a coherent, if incomplete, history. Using their information as my starting point to search places like the Maryland State Archives in the Hall of Records in Annapolis, I was able to assemble the first publication on the Quander family history. "The Quanders: Roots and Branches, a Summary" was distributed at the fourth Quanders United family reunion. It was a beautiful publication, the concerted effort of a cross section of the family. Still at only twenty-nine pages, it was not a comprehensive document. Cousin Bernard Brooks's beautiful cover for the booklet depicted a tree trunk with four large branches. Two of the branches represented the two Maryland-DC Quander groups, and the other two represented the main branches of the Virginia-Pennsylvania Quanders. None of the members of the four branches were able to explain, in 1977, how they were related to each other, a distinction that sadly remains to this day. Yet one thing is certain. Anyone who knows the family's history cannot successfully argue that the four groups are not related, as the root sources are far too strong and of such a similar nature that the notion that we are not a single extended family unit cannot fruitfully be entertained.

At our fifth reunion in 1978, we began the process of incorporation to make Quanders United a legal and more lasting entity. Among the stated purposes of the corporation were to promote within present and future family members a greater sense of appreciation for the Quander family's rich background, history, and achievements and to provide a sense of organization and continuity among family-sponsored gatherings. In spite of this effort, interest in planning and executing the Maryland-DC reunions began to wane partly because a small but steady number of Quanders United members attended the Virginia-Pennsylvania QFR. After our sixth reunion in 1979, we did not meet again until September 1982 when Quanders United gave a well-attended champagne brunch with the theme "A Time for Family History." By then, my family history research was far more comprehensive than ever before, and I had been recognized as a genealogical historian by various local organizations. When the brunch committee invited me to speak, I prepared a lecture titled "The Quander Family, 1684–1984: Its History and Its Roots." Considering that Quanders United had been in a quiet mode for three years, this successful event reassured us that interest in our family history was still strong, even if attending meetings of Quanders United, Inc. was not a favorite activity.

Just four weeks before, the QFR had enjoyed its fifty-seventh annual reunion with the theme of "Our Family Tree." Although Quanders United never intended pressuring the QFR, that is exactly what was manifesting itself. By 1982, several QFR members were openly challenging the Maryland-DC Quanders to prove there was a family connection between the two groups. No gauntlet was cast, but subtle hints were everywhere. For example, the QFR members had learned that one of my research goals was to establish, if possible, where in Africa the Quanders came from. In an apparent gibe at the notion of an African connection, the 1982 QFR program stated, "For fifty-six years, we have survived knowing that our ancestors built a strong institution with strong roots. The question is not a matter of tracing our roots back to Africa but fifty-six years to 1926 and to our relatives who started the first family reunion."

The ensuing five to six years proved challenging. Communication difficulties between the two groups were accentuated as Quanders United prepared for the family's 1984 celebration of three hundred years in the Americas. We began to realize that there was not merely disagreement but genuine animosity, emanating from a few members of the QFR, mostly older people who were the children of the original founders. Attending the Virginia-Pennsylvania reunions became increasingly unpleasant for the Maryland-DC group. The unwelcome mat was particularly noticeable in Pennsylvania. I remained convinced that the majority of the North Clan—the Pennsylvania Quanders—were open to the idea of a historical family connection. But the entrenched seniors not only held out, but also they swayed other QFR members to their hostile point of view. Quanders United was at a crossroads. We realized 1984 was rapidly approaching and with it the need to prepare for the Tricentennial Celebration, the family's single largest event to date. There had been much talk about the need to stop and reflect after three hundred years, yet no planning had been done to make the observance happen, and we were a long way from reconciling with the North Clan.

CHAPTER 9

⁺⁺⁺◆⁺⁺⁺

The Tricentennial
Celebration, 1684–1984

We had been notified in 1978 by historians from Charles County, Maryland, that the Quander family was the oldest consistently documented African American family in the county for which records survived. It was not too much of a reach to surmise that if the Quanders were the oldest such family in the original thirteen colonies, we might also be the oldest Black family in the entire United States. However, we could not verify this possibility based upon the information available. It made no difference to us, as we were not celebrating being the oldest anything, but rather having been documented in America for three hundred years. At the time, 1984 seemed far away, and we talked but didn't act. A few more years passed, and my father, James Quander, said several times, "We must do something big and memorable in 1984." Still nothing was done. Conscious of the passing time, in 1983, my dad decided to bite the bullet. He convened a planning meeting and invited the Quanders United president and vice president to attend. It was a tense gathering, but we were underway.

The first planning meeting for the Tricentennial Celebration on April 30, 1983, was only eight months before the thee-hundredth anniversary year would begin. The cross section of the family gathered that day named ourselves the "Tricentennial Steering Committee," and we immediately set about the monumental task of planning a grand three-hundred-year observance. We agreed that the events should be designed to bring national attention to the Quander family, as a three-hundred-year celebration was more than just another family reunion. This intention to make history was in sharp contrast to the history making by the Quanders who had gone before us, who unintentionally made history while going about their business. Many of us wanted the Tricentennial to be held at a location that was itself special, someplace that was also significant within the family. We voted unanimously for Howard University. Bernard Moon, the university's scheduling manager at the time, was initially incredulous about an African American family wanting to rent Blackburn Center for a Tricentennial Celebration. On the phone to my dad, Moon exclaimed, "Three hundred years! Is that really possible? Three hundred years!"

Some family objected to seeking attention. Others countered by pointing out that too often news related to African Americans is negative, so something good, such as this event, should be positively celebrated, with the world brought into our circle during this brief period. It was only a weekend, and after the celebration, we'd be back to business as usual. Other than the Quanders themselves, we thought few people would remember our celebration after a few months. That statement would prove to be wonderfully incorrect.

At that first planning meeting, we adopted a celebration theme: "Faith, Reverence, Achievement: One Family under God Our Father, with a Common Root and Many Branches." A list of suggested activities included a get-acquainted cocktail mixer, a fashion show, a semiformal dinner with entertainment, a picnic on Quander Road, a historical workshop, and an interdenominational worship service. To execute a program this ambitious would require multiple committees and planning meetings. The second planning session was held in June and the third in September.

In October, we enjoyed our fall picnic and general membership meeting at the home of Roberta H. Quander who lived on Quander Road in Alexandria, Virginia. Whenever we have an event at Roberta's, it is truly a case of "going home," as her home is one of the remaining family homesteads. The land on which the house sits is part of the eighty-eight-acre tract in Spring Bank that dairy farmer Charles Henry and Amanda Rebecca Bell Quander, Roberta's grandparents, accumulated in the 1870s. I was unanimously elected at that meeting as the third president of Quanders United. As the new president and with the weight of the Tricentennial planning on my shoulders, I resigned my post as family historian and immediately presented a proposed Quanders United Constitution and Bylaws that I had already drafted, plus an application for tax-exempt status. There was much work still to be done on planning the Tricentennial Celebration, and with only $858.28 in the treasury, the collection of dues was paramount, as well as projecting the costs of various events, so that we could at least break even on the financial outlays anticipated.

Because I knew the general membership needed to be kept informed about the Tricentennial planning, after the October meeting, I sent everyone a detailed three-page letter, a true epistle. It was the first comprehensive communication since we began planning the celebration in April, and some recipients complained it was too long for them to read. I knew the converse would have been true: people would have complained had I not informed them.

I presided over my first Tricentennial steering committee meeting in November 1983 in my Brookland home. Several key issues were discussed and important decisions made. Our tax-exempt status had been applied for with the Internal Revenue Service. A post office box was obtained, as we expected to receive a large amount of correspondence. Letterhead was ordered that listed the officers, cochairs, and steering committee members in the margin. A bulk permit was obtained for reduced postage costs in anticipation of frequent mailings. Unquestionably, all efforts had to be made to increase the Quanders United membership and participation, as there had never been a Quander event of such magnitude before.

Discussion turned to how best to fund the celebration. The consensus was that we needed to charge a modest registration fee, plus a small charge for each event, to help underwrite and spread out the total costs. We wanted to keep the charges low because there were many large families, some with young children, and if we were insensitive to their costs, many of them would elect not to participate. Everyone was committed to not letting that happen not only because we were all family but also because we believed no Quander, regardless of financial circumstances, should be excluded from this event.

Much of the discussion concerned the proposed souvenir journal. Challengers argued that the magnitude of that project was greater than both our financial and professional resources and the amount of time we had available. Supporters countered with the idea of creating a publication family and friends would cherish and be discussing for years to come. I underscored that my objective was to create a sense of deep historical connection to the early family roots in Maryland, Virginia, and Washington, DC. We asked the it-can't-be-done group, "If you cannot muster enough support to publish a Quander family history on our three-hundredth anniversary, then when can you do it?" We envisioned a well-researched, artistically presented historical statement, fully illustrated with family photographs, which would unify Quanders everywhere, giving us a sense of history, place, pride, and connection. In addition, an *In Memoriam* section of appreciation and recognition of various ancestors would remind us all their contributions and make them a part of the celebration.

Challengers were eventually won over to the idea that there was no better and lasting means of documenting the family's three-hundredth anniversary celebration than the souvenir journal. Eventually, we agreed that the steering committee members, as well as other interested family members, would solicit advertisements from individuals, churches, community groups, and local and national organizations that might want to congratulate us while promoting their product or service or simply be listed as sponsors.

With Thanksgiving and Christmas approaching, I elected to keep everyone informed by mail. Again, there were some complaints about the letters being too long with too many details. But I resolved to keep up the correspondence and urged the membership to keep everything in an information file for quick reference.

Between March and May 1984, there was a scurrying about for information to put into the souvenir journal. The long and detailed letter I sent in February explaining what an invaluable tool the journal would be seemed to have done the trick. More and more family and friends contributed bits and pieces of Quander information, and we determined to try our best to fit every bit of it into a section called *Did You Know?* Making the journal a success took the concerted action of a large group, and thank goodness, they came forward. Kenny Brown coordinated the overall effort of securing and coordinating information and arranging the layout, and Carmen handled all the artistic components, including drawing the cover art and creating six drawings related to some aspect of the family's notable history. We had already distributed advertising agreements for potential advertisers and forms for sponsors to complete and return. My telephone rang constantly with questions about the journal.

As my letters found their intended mark, the excitement and anticipation grew, and more and more documents and photographs began to show up. I received an M Street High School (forerunner of Dunbar High School) activity program for 1899, which listed Susie Quander as a member of the Class of 1900. Photographs taken more than one hundred years ago were located that had been tucked away, almost forgotten, and—in some cases—actually forgotten. More than once, nineteenth-century Quander-related photos were presented with the apologetic statement, "I don't know who this is." In some cases, we were able to identify the subjects but not always.

Negatives were created of many of the photographs, as I already had the idea of preserving them in a central repository in an organization that would later be known as the Quander Historical Society, Inc. Family members were encouraged to let down their modesty and tell us about themselves and what people in their sector of the family had done. Great emphasis was also placed upon the current generation, both youth and adults, as they were tomorrow's ancestors. We urged individuals to submit something about themselves in writing, as well as current photographs, to help the steering committee build a bridge from the past to the future via the present.

With a few exceptions, all the documents and photographs were promptly returned. One portrait sustained damage when its old frame disintegrated. We replaced it at the committee's cost. Unfortunately, two photographs were lost, probably initially misidentified, and were never returned to their lenders. Although the steering committee took responsibility for the lost items, the blame and wrath fell upon me, as I was the prime mover to separate the photographs from their owners. As would be expected, the anxiety associated with the loss was expressed sevenfold. No amount of apology or acceptance of responsibility was sufficient, although I never sought to lessen the importance of the loss attached by the original owners. The good news in both instances was that the two lenders each had another copy of the lost photo, which information they withheld until after they finished dressing me down to their satisfaction.

The closer we got to the third week of June, the more events picked up. Two important congratulations were received on April 10, 1984. On that day, DC Delegate Walter Fauntroy placed a "Tribute to the Quander Family" in the U.S. *Congressional Record* that outlined the family's distinguished history of contributions to the local and larger communities. Fauntroy noted, "Strong family ties should be commended as a model for our youth and the community at large. The Quander Family [has] toiled in many vineyards through the centuries, and made meaningful contributions in each, and thus in the future of our Nation." He concluded by inviting his colleagues in the U.S. House of Representatives to join him in saluting the Quander family. On that same day, the Council of the District of Columbia passed "The Quander Family Tricentennial Resolution of 1984," which was presented to all assembled family members two days later in the District Building.

By mid-April, the steering committee was moving into high gear. The treasury had begun to swell, as proceeds were received for the display ads, patron and sponsor greetings, *In Memorium*, and the banquet tickets. The banquet committee expected between three hundred and five hundred people at the Saturday, June 23 evening banquet, which would include time for socialization, a meal, and a full program of speakers and entertainment. The banquet committee also organized a get-acquainted fashion show for Friday evening, June 22, at which family art, artifacts, heirlooms, photographs, and the four-part Quander family tree were to be presented and displayed.

A major publicity undertaking had been completed, with 125 press releases sent to local and national organizations, including the *Washington Post*, the *Afro American*, and *Ebony* magazine, plus the major television networks and radio stations. Invitations to the banquet had been sent to President and Mrs. Ronald Reagan, Governor Harold Hughes of Maryland, Governor Charles Robb of Virginia, Mayor Marion Barry of Washington, DC, Congressman Walter Fauntroy, and a host of other political and religious leaders. Although most of the dignitaries invited extended regrets at not attending, many of them sent letters of greeting for inclusion in the souvenir journal, and Mayor Barry's office notified us that June 17–24, 1984, would be declared "Quander Week" in the District of Columbia. Responses from the media were slower to arrive, although the *Washington Times* interviewed my father and me about the family's history.

During this busy time, we dealt with three issues in addition to planning for the Tricentennial weekend. There had long been talk that we needed to create our own coat of arms, something that would be meaningful to us as Quanders and African Americans. Some family members rejected Afrocentrism and had reservations about adopting anything that was "too African." Generally, however, the feeling was that we were of African origin and we should not lose sight of where our ancestors came from. Although we all were of mixed racial ancestry, the European part of our gene pool was, for the most past, a component we did not necessarily know or celebrate. But we did know something of our Ghanaian ancestry, and the more general African-based heritage that was a familiar part of our family culture, friendships, and associations was a lifelong experience. The consensus was that we need not be concerned about sticking to any European rules of heraldry but rather to make our own choices based upon what was relevant to our Quander history.

The second issue, which was closely related to the first, concerned our growing interest in our African past. Having had clues for decades about Ghana being the most logical place of origin and the Ghanaian Akan language naming system being the source of the Quander surname, I had contacted the Ghanaian Embassy in Washington, DC, in mid-1983. I was directed to Ebenezer Ackwetta, who was effusive in asserting that "Quander" was most certainly of Ghanaian origin. He noted that the Quander surname, or some variation of it, still existed in Ghana. I was reminded of how students from Ghana at Howard University in the 1960s invariably called me Mr. Quando and told me my surname was not "Quander" but "Amaquandoh."

Following Mr. Ackwetta's suggestion, I wrote to the weekly *Mirror* and the *People's Daily Graphic*, two prominent newspapers in Ghana, inquiring whether their readers could provide information about the "Quander" and "Amaquandoh" surnames. The full letter, including my address and telephone number, appeared on the front page of the *Mirror* on December 10, 1983, under the banner, "American Family in Search of Its Roots." The article set off a torrent of letters from Ghana. I was overwhelmed with the number of responses, even collect telephone calls, each purporting to provide some family-related information.

One afternoon in late January 1984, my telephone rang. The caller, Joseph Kojo Amaquandoh, explained that he lived in New York but had just returned from Ghana and was contacting me at the express directive of the elders from the village of Kankaboom, Cape Coast, Ghana. I invited him and his brother, Ernest Kweku Amaquandoh, to visit the following weekend and hastily assembled the steering committee and a cross section of other family members to come to my house to meet them. The Amaquandoh brothers discussed Ghanaian history and customs and verified that even in Ghana the name Amaquandoh had been Anglicized, and sometimes appeared as Quander, just as the embassy staff had said.

In early April, I again had a call from New York. Ernest Kweku Amaquandoh explained that several members of the Ghana-based Amaquandoh clan wanted to attend the Tricentennial Celebration and asked if there was anything we could do to make that happen. This request caught me by total surprise. Obviously, they had no concept of how difficult it would be to achieve such a result. Visas would have to be obtained; airfare would have to be raised. Accommodations would have to be provided for our guests, probably at our expense. Most likely, our Ghanaian counterparts assumed we were rich and could easily arrange for them to come for the celebration. The task proved impossible to achieve but not before we had spent precious time politely wrangling with the Immigration and Naturalization Service about securing visas for approximately twenty-five Ghanaians; discussing whether we could, would, or should file affidavits of support for our proposed visitors, all whom were complete strangers; and contacting local slaughterhouses about where we could secure a live sheep or goat and whether it was legal to kill it in the backyard of our Brookland home. The Amaquandohs from Ghana would have enriched the Tricentennial, but they also would have completely altered our American celebration.

However, one Ghanaian did attend the Tricentennial Celebration. We received a call from the Embassy of Ghana that His Excellency Eric Otoo, Ghanaian ambassador to the United States, would attend the Tricentennial banquet as our guest. Could he first meet with me and my father? I was delighted and arranged for the ambassador and Mr. Ackwetta, the Ghanaian consul, to visit my home. Mr. Otoo stated how pleased he was to have met us and that he looked forward to attending the Tricentennial. He encouraged us to follow up with the connection between the American Quanders and the Ghanaian Amaquandohs.

The third issue was predictable, yet its vehemence took us by surprise. Having secured the addresses of several of the Virginia-Pennsylvania group, Quanders United invited them to take part in the Tricentennial Celebration. We learned later that the older QFR members insisted that no one was to speak to anyone from Quanders United, give us any information, or participate in the upcoming celebration. Although our letters were largely ignored, a few Virginia Quanders embraced the events, and eventually, word about the celebration got back to the Pennsylvania Quanders. Having elected to ignore our initial invitations and likewise not fully appreciating the magnitude of what we were undertaking, they were incensed about a three-hundredth anniversary celebration that did not seem to include them. Claiming they were the original Quanders and we were merely upstarts trying to upstage them and their special place in history, including the Mount Vernon-George Washington connection, many of them became furious about the impending Tricentennial events. We were met with disdain and rebuff by many of the Pennsylvania and a few of the Virginian Quanders who insisted that in the absence of definitive proof of a sanguine connection, they would not accept that the Maryland-DC Quanders were even distantly related to them. To replies that the connection was certain, due to the similar history, continuous use of the same first names, and other recognizable factors, the naysayers retorted with further unsupported denials.

The initial letters about the Tricentennial had been sent to the few QFR members for whom we had addresses. Most of the Virginia-Pennsylvania group did not know we had tried to reach them but had been blocked by those people who had received the letters, who unilaterally decided that the rest of the Quanders would not be participating. But how do you explain that just before the celebration begins? How do you convince this other group that we wanted them to be a part of the event but that their most senior members refused to share contact information with us? Interpreting their combination of no response or hostile responses as a lack of interest, we elected to not continue sending invitations and requests for information, which we believed would only add to the hostility. Even so, many Pennsylvania Quanders renounced some of their Virginia counterparts for cozying up to the Maryland-DC group and insisted they had to choose whether to remain with the original 1926 QFR or select a new affiliation.

Several of the Virginia descendants and their spouses refused to choose sides. They sincerely believed there was a connection, reinforced by the fact that Charles Henry Quander was born a slave (c. 1840), allegedly in or around Bladensburg, Maryland, and was transported to Virginia as a child. Gladys Quander Tancil, his granddaughter, was called a traitor, untrustworthy, and with severely divided loyalties. Gladys was deeply offended by these accusations, but she refused to choose a side. Doris Davis Quander, widow of Emmett D. Quander, a founder of Quanders United, wrote a letter in April 1984 entreating everyone to be more open-minded about the family link between the different Quander groups and encouraging the Virginia-Pennsylvania group to join in the celebration. Doris was mostly ignored by the Pennsylvania folk, but sparked by her letter, a few more Virginia Quanders signed up to celebrate. And despite the urging from the Pennsylvania group to boycott the event, a handful from the North Clan sent in their registration fees.

While the fury of the inclusion issue raged, the plans for the event still needed to be carried out. On May 5, 1984, only six weeks before the grand event, the general membership met. One of the main agenda items was the adoption of the Quander coat of arms. As president, I recounted the significance of each item on the proposed coat of arms. The main colors—red, yellow, and green—are the colors of Ghana. The wings symbolize flight, meaning that each of us can soar as high and far as we possibly can in life. The two white-breasted black ravens facing away from each other symbolize both the original separation of the African Amkwandohs from their American cousins and the separation of the two brothers after their arrival in the Maryland colony. Initially, there had been disagreement about the raven because it looked like a crow, which, to many older family members, was reminiscent of "Jim Crow" and racial segregation in this country. We decided to use the raven, the national bird of Ghana, and make certain it was always identified as such.

The mortarboard is a symbol of education, as the family has a history of being teachers and pursuing higher education, and the braided "Q," of course, represents our surname. The cocoa leaves, green on the top and red on the bottom, symbolize Ghana, life and hope, and the struggle we sometimes must bear, even to the shedding of blood. The helmet with a cross symbolizes Christianity and the Ten Commandments, as we learned that, like the Quanders in America, the Ghanaian Amaquandohs are predominantly Christian. The four parts of the shield contain a rake and hoe, symbolic farm instruments; a cow, again symbolic of agriculture; a chain broken in two, with a part rejoined to symbolize released shackles and the different parts of the family being reunited; and a ship on blue water showing the crossing of the family from Africa to America and, once here, the crossing of the Potomac River from Maryland to Virginia. At the bottom of the shield are the words, "We Are Many, but We Are One."

Faced with looming publication deadlines, I also turned my attention to completing the souvenir journal. I wrote a twenty-page essay, "The History of the Quander Family," taking care to footnote it for historical accuracy. The journal's text was complemented by Carmen's drawings, three of which were from the Maryland-DC history, and three from the Virginia-Pennsylvania side of the family. Carmen created two additional drawings, one for the journal cover and the other a map indicating the proximity of the Mount Vernon estate to Wheeler's Folly in Maryland, part of which Henry Quando obtained in 1695 in his ninety-nine-year freehold lease.

Carmen pursued this ambitious project with enthusiasm, but her progress was abruptly and sadly interrupted when her brother Raul died suddenly, barely three days before the publication deadline. Carmen's parents were long divorced, and Raul, who was ten years older than Carmen, had served as a surrogate father. In her mind, her father had died, and with the pressures associated with having to make funeral arrangements, complete the artwork, and get everything to the printer in camera-ready form, she hardly had time to grieve. Although I never would have abandoned Carmen at such an emotional time, my concern for her was coupled with overseeing the finalization of the celebration. She naturally questioned my priorities, to which I could only reply that I was trying to balance everything at the same time, and I was deeply sorry if there was simply not enough emotional support and time to get everything done within the rapidly dwindling time remaining. By now, I was losing sleep. I had taken to keeping a memo pad at my bedside to write down notes when I awoke in the middle of the night. I was writing memos to everyone, creating and providing checklists at every turn, and constantly measuring progress. Despite the stresses and strains of the moment, we pressed on, and gradually, almost everything was accomplished.

Then suddenly, almost overnight, it seemed we were just about there. As promised, Mayor Barry declared June 17–24, 1984, as "Quander Week" in the District of Columbia. June 17 was also Trinity Sunday, on which St. Augustine Catholic Church, founded in 1858, celebrates its annual homecoming. Originally located on

Fifteenth Street, the old cathedral was erected in the 1870s by African Americans, many of whom had been enslaved. After many years of service, in 1946, the church building was sold to the *Washington Post*. Church staff and *Post* officials had decided to place a historical marker commemorating the old church on the front of the *Post* building. The priests and parish council wanted the marker to be unveiled by someone with established ties to the church. James and Eunice Quander Taylor, lifelong members of the parish, were selected.

Alerted to James and Eunice's role on the same day that began Quander Week, the family attended mass in significant numbers. Afterward, the entire congregation marched down the middle of Fifteenth Street, which was closed off by the police. It was a colorful event with hundreds marching to the old site. We held a brief ceremony in front of the *Washington Post* building, followed by James and Eunice unveiling the commemorative bronze plaque. Dr. Vince Reed, vice president of the *Post*, warmly greeted us and noted that Eunice was a member of "that historic Quander family," which was celebrating three hundred documented years in America. All doubt was removed at that moment. The Tricentennial Celebration had begun.

The celebration had begun, but preparations continued. Family genealogy information continued to pour in during that final week. I had divided the four main branches of the Quander family into groupings, as many of us still did not know where we fit into the family tree. An extended family chart would give everyone a sense of place. A huge amount of information needed to be quickly assembled and displayed to let everyone see the progress we had made, as well as to elicit additional information.

During the week before the celebration, several local radio stations—including WMAL, WRC, WYCB, WHUR, and WUST, and even a few out-of-town stations—had interviewed me. The public's interest in the events was greatly sparked by these two-to-three-minute interviews, some of which were live telephone conversations. A few strangers called my house to ask if they could attend the events. I explained that the Tricentennial Celebration was a culmination of a long planning cycle, a time for Quanders to come together and be family. I wanted to believe that most of the callers understood and respected my wishes that they not attend, but I soon learned otherwise.

Trying to secure an advance commitment from the *Washington Post* to cover the celebration had proved difficult. "We'll see," they told us. "Generally, we don't cover family reunions, but this one looks a little different. We'll let you know." Conversely, the Washington *Afro American* called me at home to schedule an interview. The result was a moving page one story that captured our excitement, pride, and humility at being the family blessed in so many ways. Noting that the Quanders boast doctors and lawyers, the article gave equal respect to family members who worked as beauticians and unskilled laborers. I was quoted as saying, "Sure, we have our share of gangsters and crooks, but I think that you will find that we're very humble and have not forgotten our roots. Despite slavery and other drawbacks, we still have managed to survive."

Quanders gather at Howard University,
Washington, DC, during Tricentennial
Celebration(1684-1984), June 1984

The celebration weekend finally arrived. I had been working at the DC government's Department of Employment Services, plus maintaining a small private law practice on the side. Both suffered greatly during the final weeks of preparation, as the effort of making everything just right was all-consuming. To try to catch my breath for the opening of the three-day event, I didn't go into work on Friday, June 22. It was the correct decision. At about 9:00 a.m., my telephone rang. WRC television, our local NBC affiliate, had decided to cover the Tricentennial Celebration all three days, and they wanted to make the Quander family the lead story for the 6:00 p.m. evening news. Could I assemble the entire family at Blackburn Center by 5:45 p.m.? I was in shock! This was the first day of the celebration, and until the day before, I was uncertain whether we would have any television coverage. Now I was being asked to assemble everyone almost an hour early. No e-mails, no text messages, no cell phones! Thank God for the telephone tree, which we had established some months prior.

It was a mad frenzy. We activated the tree and reached virtually everybody. Schedules were changed. Transportation plans were modified. The activities coordinators were advised that whatever their respective plans for the evening were, they would have to be sped up to be operational by 5:45 p.m. Within the hour, several additional calls came from news media, likewise requesting that we assemble for the 6:00 p.m. evening news. WNBC Channel 4 sent Joe Johns, who expanded our local coverage to national scope through WNBC New York. The local ABC affiliate sent two teams. Jeanne Meserve, a nationally and later internationally accredited news journalist, represented ABC national news; while Sam Ford, then a local news reporter, represented WJLA Channel 7 local news. By the end of the weekend, the family reunion that many of the press initially indicated they probably would not cover grew into a major national-level news cycle.

Family began arriving by 5:30 p.m., positioning themselves on the second floor in the Blackburn Center lounge. The media trucks were in place, ready to report live at 6:00 p.m. As president, I was asked by all the networks to talk to them first, but as it was impossible to be in more than one place at the stroke of 6:00 p.m., the times were staggered, although by only a few minutes. First, I interviewed with Channel 4, as they called first and initiated this mad rush. All networks asked essentially the same questions, most typically, "What does it feel like to be a Quander?" and, "How do you feel today knowing what you ancestors endured for so long that now makes it possible for you to be here today to celebrate this grand series of events?"

The evening was a deep and moving experience, one that everyone in the family shared. The media conducted interview after interview, using clips on the nightly eleven-o'clock news. Deep down inside, we all visualize ourselves as celebrities. The minutes of individualized fame gave those of us who were interviewed a sense that out in the world there really was an interest in family in general and in the Quander family in particular. Several of the cousins who were interviewed were over eighty years of age. I vividly recall their pride as they related their life stories, their parents' lives, and how pleased they were to be present that June evening when the whole nation stopped to give recognition to the Quander family.

The heirlooms, art, and artifacts lent by the family were displayed on tables, and photographs were mounted on easels. Carmen, a trained artist and museum curator, received all items in advance, and used her artistic handwriting to capture relevant information. Who is depicted in this photograph? What is this item, and what is its significance? Who lent the item? Who did the item belong to originally? Using this approach, the shawls of several ancestral women were displayed, as were some of their dishware and personal handicrafts. Carmen also framed her original artwork for the souvenir journal and displayed it as the "Quando Collection."

That evening, I premiered the four branches of the Quander family tree I had been so feverishly working on. With so many last-minute things to do, the task proved not only daunting but also largely impossible to complete. Still the effort was important as it was the first time anyone had attempted to show the four main branches of the family and how most of us fit into the family tree. It was comical in some instances to see a family draw up to the display and look for themselves. I heard more than one say, "That date is not correct!" or, "They left out a child!" Because the information was intentionally written in pencil on white foam board, it could be easily erased and corrected. Pencils were provided to make adjustments on the tree if space permitted, and scratch paper was provided for longer corrections. Each viewer was asked to correct misinformation and add the names and birth and death years of missed family members. One prominent family member erased her birth year. When I chided her that she was defacing a historical document, she retorted, "It's not anyone else's business how old I am!"

We had elected to tell everybody about our celebration when we issued the press releases, and we were naïve not to realize that a few television viewers and radio listeners would crash the party. Less than two hours from when we began, I saw we had been joined by both strangers and people I knew, none of whom were Quanders or invited guests. Having seen the event featured on the 6:00 p.m. news, they simply showed up, excited at being a part of the Quander family, if only for one evening. These party crashers mixed and mingled, ate and drank, and joined in the rapture of the moment. A few were even interviewed by the press! I overhead one of them tell a reporter he wished he had been blessed with a large historic family, but that at least for this evening, he was a Quander too.

By 10:00 p.m., the group was disbursing. As I tried to wind down from the adrenaline high I had been on for the prior twenty-four hours, I thought of the many northern Quander family members who had refused to participate in this historic event, and I realized the loss was truly theirs. Later, as events unfolded and they came to appreciate the magnitude of the celebration they had missed, several expressed deep regret at having been misled by other family members who swayed their decision not to participate.

Carmen and I were home in time to catch the 11:00 p.m. news. Despite the hour, our telephone rang repeatedly as our friends, many of whom had no idea of the depth of this special celebration, called to congratulate us or ask how we managed to orchestrate such a special event. The Tricentennial Celebration was a lead story at both the 6:00 p.m. and 11:00 p.m. news and remained so for the entire weekend. As Channel 4's Joe Johns said to me, "You guys have been really lucky! There wasn't much news this weekend, so the Quander story is the big story of the hour." He covered the story all three days.

Registration for family members continued on Saturday morning at the Blackburn Center, and the general public was invited to see our history, art, artifacts, and genealogy display. Each registration kit contained a souvenir journal. However, many outside visitors wanted the high-quality, glossy 102-page journal, and we sold individual copies. The demand outstripped the seven hundred journals we had printed, so after the celebration, we ordered a second printing to accommodate the continuing interest.

The highlight of Saturday morning was a general membership meeting of Quanders United. The meeting was largely an open forum. My father, a Quanders United founder, was so filled with joy and emotion he could hardly speak. He told of how many years ago he had wondered why he did not know many of his Quander relatives, which he attributed in part to his own father, John Edward Quander (1883–1950), having been orphaned at an early age. The concept of family intimacy was diluted when his father and his siblings were divided up among other relatives. He reminded everyone that today was Quander Day, and this was a celebration of what it meant "To Be a Quander!"

For that evening's banquet in Blackburn Center's grand ballroom, Carmen had hand painted a twenty-foot-wide banner proclaiming "Quanders United" with the coat of arms boldly displayed between the two words. The banner, which was hung behind the elevated head table, appeared all over the United States in the media's print and news broadcasts. Each of the speakers addressed some aspect of family values and how pleased they were to be a part of this special celebration, encouraging us to continue to serve as role models for families everywhere, regardless of race, religion, or national origin.

Although many of the Quanders present that evening were Catholic, the service the following morning was Christian but non-denominational. The presiding minister was Rev. Frederick Barnes, a direct descendant of Nancy Carter Quander and senior minister of the African Methodist Episcopal Zion Church. As sunlight filtered through the impressive stained glass windows of the Andrew Rankin Chapel at Howard University, ABC national television filmed the service, which ran as a featured story on the 11:00 p.m. Sunday news. The evening news program closed with Quanders United founder Eunice Q. Taylor, the former lead soloist from the St. Augustine choir, singing praises to her God, giving thanks for the many bountiful blessings we all received that famed weekend.

Our Sunday afternoon picnic was interrupted by a heavy downpour, and although we couldn't conclude our fabulous weekend at one of the family's historic homesteads, we moved indoors to the basement of the St. Augustine Church School, which was itself a historically significant site. But as Channel 4's Joe Johns noted, the only thing damp was the weather, as our spirits were not in any way dampened as the celebration wound down to its successful conclusion.

After the celebration of the century, nothing much could be said that was not anticlimactic. We had our memories, our newspaper clippings, and an ensured place in history. And we had joined together in ways that had never occurred, and sadly, may never reach that level of love, spirituality, and friendship again. I concluded my personal celebration with a great hope that something lasting would emerge and be sustained, that all the components of the Quander family would come together and truly be united, rather than split by the continued fractious behavior from certain sectors. Even after the Tricentennial Celebration, some Quander relatives continued to deny or question whether the branches of the family were truly related. Sometimes, the best thing to do is nothing, and that was the consensus of the Maryland-DC Quanders: ignore the naysayers in the Virginia-Pennsylvania part of the family for now, and let time and common sense imprint their marks. Indeed, the naysayers were already decreasing. I took their refusals to talk to me—which went as far as having people hang up the telephone as soon as I identified myself—in stride and was not dissuaded from my objectives.

The newspapers were generous in publishing the details of the weekend celebration. On Monday, June 25, 1984, "Black Family Celebrates 300-Year Maryland Roots" headlined page one of the main section of the *Washington Post*. A few days later, the Prince George's County *Sentinel* published "Oldest County Family Unites," in which local officials recognized that the Tricentennial showed "the city, the country, and the whole world that Washington is more than a conglomerate of people who came and go every four years. It is a community."

The big event was over. It was time to unwind. But the next day and in the days following my return to work, I was interrupted constantly by well-wishers and people wanting to know how we managed to pull off such a major event and how they could begin to research their own family history. The ink of the next few days' newspapers was hardly dry when a new era of the Quander story had begun.

CHAPTER 10

The Quanders Begin Their
Fourth Century

Despite the family's need to relax from the excitement of the Tricentennial weekend and get back to business as usual, the public recognition and enthusiasm about the celebration at Howard University was far from over. The weekly newspapers carried the story into early July, reporting that the Quander family was unusual for a number of reasons, not only for their ability to trace their roots back so many generations. The *Catholic Standard* noted our sustained connection to Catholicism, which was atypical for an African American family. Later in the summer, cousin Sandra Rattley released "The Quanders: A Tricentennial Celebration," which was heard on National Public Radio across the nation. It was the first of several documentaries and included an excellent cross section of Quander family interviews, including her grandmother, Helen O. Stewart Quander (1901–2001), and Tricentennial cochair Roberta H. Quander. Grasping the importance of the family's precious history and its collective knowledge bank, the Smithsonian Institution, through Dr. Bernice Johnson Reagon, director of the museum's Program of Black American Culture, contacted the family and requested the opportunity to interview senior family members for an oral history project. Suddenly, relatives who never thought of themselves as such became "experts." I had been working on accumulating

THE QUANDERS—SINCE 1684,
AN ENDURING AFRICAN AMERICAN LEGACY

our family history since 1968, when I attended my first Quander reunion. Now it seemed the world was beating a path to our door. I was always willing to share what I knew, and I encouraged family members to take an interest in developing an awareness and appreciation about our distinguished history. I have met with mixed results, often the result of their not wanting to toot the family horn. But on this occasion, several older family members, still basking in the light of the Tricentennial, were at least temporarily willing to talk.

The steering committee agreed we needed a debriefing to discuss what had transpired during the Tricentennial Celebration weekend and to consider what we should do next. Attendance was small at that September 1984 meeting, perhaps thirty people. This small turnout was typical of the way Quanders United had operated prior to the big event, and now we had quickly reverted to that routine. The waning of enthusiasm was also obvious in many of the final reports, which were oral rather than written as requested. The overall consensus at the debriefing was that although the Tricentennial Celebration was a magnificent occasion and everyone was glad to have participated, the media focus and overall attention were given to too few people and should have been more equally distributed among family members. No one specifically indicated I was the target of this criticism due to my constant interview requests from the media, but everyone there knew the remarks were directed against me personally.

I responded that I could not tell the media who to talk to. If journalists asked for the oldest present Quander-born women, I directed them to Henrietta Q. Walls. If they wanted to talk to the steering committee, I directed them to cochairs Roberta and Paul (Roberta H. Quander and Paul A. Quander Jr.). But inevitably, the interview questions turned to family history, and I had the most comprehensive and diversified knowledge of Quander family history. But never, even as this chapter is being written, have I laid claim to an exclusive right to that history. I asked them then, and I still ask, what is the responsibility within the family to gather and preserve our history so all may share it for generations to come? The situation, unfortunately, remains pretty much the same. With a few exceptions, most likely, much of the history will die with me unless I commit it to writing. It's up to me not to drop the ball. Some people were still unhappy about my seeming to get so much media attention, but the meeting resumed after my explanation.

We remained concerned about the general nonparticipation of our Virginia-Pennsylvania cousins. At that time, we still did not know the extent of the older QFR members' directive that the Virginia-Pennsylvania group should refuse to talk to us. Given the rumblings about alleged exclusion, even some Maryland-DC family expressed reservations about holding our annual Quanders United picnic on Quander Road, in the heart of Virginia Quander territory. After discussing the matter, we all agreed we had done nothing wrong, had not deliberately excluded anyone, and indeed had reached out to them as well as we could have given our lack of contact information.

Discussion at the Quanders United picnic later that September continued to focus on the QFR response to the Tricentennial weekend. They too had held a debriefing during their fifty-ninth annual reunion the month before. Allegedly, their discussions grew acrimonious as they asked, "Who are these people claiming to be Quanders, and how could they have held a three-hundredth anniversary celebration without us?" and, "If there really is a connection between the Maryland-DC people and us, why didn't we hear about them from our grandparents when we were growing up?" Some of the Virginia-Pennsylvania group continued to stridently deny any familial relationship. Their assertion not only defied logic and evidence, it stymied subsequent efforts to elucidate family connections. Not surprisingly, research that showed the Virginia-Pennsylvania lines were not the original lines but rather offshoots from across the Potomac River in Maryland was angrily rejected.

Letters were written, generally accredited to the North Clan, questioning the feasibility of continuing the annual QFR given that several Virginia Quanders had elected to abandon the original reunion in favor of an event sponsored by upstarts. The pain, hurt, and anger—and also the misunderstanding—came through each word of these letters, as well as the desire to rupture any bonds that might have formed between the Quanders of Virginia and the

Maryland-DC group. Many of the latter, myself included, were already friendly with our Virginia counterparts and had known them for several decades, although we had rarely been a part of the QFR.

My thought was that several Virginia Quanders took temporary leave of their senses, losing sight of the history of how the QFR did not initially include every Virginia cousin until 1930, the fifth reunion. Even then, the more distant cousins were only invited to share dessert. While this controversy continued to simmer, the rest of us continued with our Tricentennial Celebration. Everyone agreed with my suggestion that October 13, 1984, three hundred years to the day that Henry Adams penned his last will and testament providing for the freedom of Henry Quander and Margrett Pugg (later Henry's wife), should not go unmarked. In contrast to the excitement and publicity of the Tricentennial Celebration weekend in June, the private October convocation to mark our first documented appearance in the New World was deeply moving, an event designed to help us reflect upon the events of the year. We needed to reassert ourselves to be more family oriented and aware of ourselves as Quanders.

We met that morning in the Quander Room at St. Benedict the Moor Catholic Church in Washington, DC. After my dad delivered the invocation, I read aloud those portions of Adams's will that reflected his intent to grant our forebears their freedom. I asked family to recall what had happened over the centuries and noted we had come this far by faith, hope, and love. Our ancestors have in part been rediscovered, I said, and we have an opportunity to appreciate the contributions of forebears with the Amkwandoh, Quando, and Quander surnames by placing documented facts and stories in a narrative that demonstrates how these men and women in seventeenth-century America and later were of great dignity and strength. They had no sense of how history would remember them. Life was hard, and their focus was on daily survival. Being Black in America was difficult and still is. They lived when there were no civil rights laws. Even when the Constitution was created, the U.S. Supreme Court ruled it did not apply to them. But they stood up for themselves anyway, and in the face of interminable racism, they claimed their rights, sought redress, and worked to see that no one took unfair advantage of their color, their poverty, or their lack of education. By standing up for themselves, they paved the way for us and created a legacy in the court, land, probate, and tax records for us to locate and interpret.

We concluded by pouring a libation, which is an act in which people, most frequently of African ancestry, come together and pour a liquid, often water or wine, onto the ground while offering prayers. I poured libation in memory of Apprendontwe, the alleged father of Egya Edoum Amkwandoh, believed to be the family forebear; Henry Quando and Margrett Pugg Quando; and to the memory of Benjamin, the undocumented "lost brother" from the story of the two brothers whose children managed to reestablish and maintain a familial bond through the centuries. I also recognized the many Quandos and Quanders who have made significant contributions through the generations.

While not wishing to prolong our consideration of the past, we recognized that in the past lies the route to the future. Perhaps three hundred years from now, in 2284, our family will look back six hundred years and appreciate what we have done to this point to document, preserve, and celebrate family to benefit future generations. I asked everyone present to draw a circle in their minds, to reflect on the eve of the beginning of our fourth century. Many Quanders spoke and gave thanks.

Kofi Nevis, a Fanti man from Ghana who was our special guest at the convocation, brought greetings from Ghanaians everywhere and noted that God made possible the seemingly impossible. He appreciated the obstacles that confronted the Quander family as we researched our history but pointed out how well our efforts paid off, helping us to establish links between African Americans and Africans who remained in Africa. Nevis related that in 1978, he had taken six African Americans to a slave castle in Kumasi, Ghana, to observe the harsh conditions where the ancestors were kept in captivity. The visitors were overcome with grief, and each wept upon seeing the place and beginning to understand the struggles those prior generations had experienced, including the terrible conditions of the ocean transport, in which many perished and only the strong survived.

Nevis's story focused our attention on who African Americans really are: descendants of the strong survivors who lived to tell about their experiences.

When concluding the special convocation, I underscored the many contributions of diverse family members who worked tirelessly to make the Tricentennial a success, recognizing that it took a collective effort to create the desired result.

But we still weren't finished. Any thought that the Tricentennial Celebration was over was premature. During this same week, Radio France International came to my home and conducted a full interview in English, for broadcast in Europe and Africa, seeking a more complete story of who the Quanders were and why we celebrated, and the significance of having such events. During that interview, I sought to dispel some preconceived notions about African Americans that many mistakenly accept as the truth, including that we have no history to speak of or worth preserving and passing on to younger generations. Within a few days of the Radio France interview, the Banneker-Douglass Museum in Annapolis, Maryland, requested that I set up a Quander photographic display and deliver a lecture on the family's distinguished and long-standing history, coupled with details on how we planned the Tricentennial Celebration.

While many accolades were coming in the Quander family's direction, the winds of dissent from the other direction had not let up. The questions concerning family connections between the two groups continued, even though some light was beginning to emerge from a few North Clan cousins who conceded that—just perhaps— we were distantly related. Partly in response to the success of the upstarts and seeing incorporation as a possible way to ensure their continued existence, in 1985, the QFR incorporated, with the stated purpose of promoting within the present and future generations of Quanders, a greater sense of appreciation of the rich history and achievements of family members. I suspect the new legal status was intended to help fend off their own feelings of insecurity and having been, in their minds, subjected to disrespect by not having been included in the Tricentennial Celebration.

Ignoring or forgetting that the first four reunions did not include the descendants of Charles Henry Quander, dairy farmer, and that this latter group was not invited to the QFR until 1930, the articles of incorporation limited membership in the organization to persons who were directly descended from the original 1926 QFR founders. Gladys Q. Tancil spoke out against the rush to incorporate largely because she knew a major misunderstanding was the driving force behind the desire to emphasize separateness. But in a mixture of anger and confusion, the hastily drafted articles of incorporation and bylaws were adopted. Gladys was already a pariah for her support of the Tricentennial Celebration, and now she was vilified for her unwavering assertion of a family connection. It was distressing to learn of the depth of separation that prevailed between us and the QFR. I asked Gladys what I, as president of Quanders United, could do to foster a solution. Sadly, she replied there was little anyone could do at the moment, given the determination of the people who were in charge and fanning the dissent. Almost in tears, she said, "You know, since 1930, I have taken an active part in this reunion. Now I have been called a traitor and verbally abused both to my face and behind my back. My only goal was to get people to see that all Quanders are related, even if distantly, but instead of listening to common sense, a small group has everyone riled up."

By early 1985, Gladys became inactive with the Virginia-Pennsylvania QFR and remained so for several years. She suggested that I should not attend any QFR events in Virginia, and she was adamant that I not attend any Pennsylvania-based reunions. The two most unwelcomed persons at any Pennsylvania Quander family events would be my dad and me, the people most identified with Quanders United and the Tricentennial Celebration. Like Gladys, my father lamented that all he ever tried to do was to build a bridge between the QFR group and Quanders United. Instead of building the bridge, he observed that if anything, he had knocked it down. Although I heeded Gladys's advice to stay away for a while, I had no intention of permanently ignoring what had been a developing relationship. But the gap between the two groups seemed to be wider than ever. What to do? What to do?

After our last event of the Tricentennial year, a Christmas party at the end of December, it seemed things would finally quiet down. But I began receiving telephone calls from individuals, organizations, and federal agencies requesting me to address their groups during Black History Month in February 1985. I accepted all the invitations, as I believed it important to get the messages of family and history across to whatever audience I could. I concentrated on making my history presentations as interesting as possible, inspirational even. Most of my audiences were friendly and receptive, but occasionally, I encountered envious challengers. More than once, I was reminded that my family wasn't alone in having a history. In addition to the slide presentations and artifacts I often brought to illustrate my talks, I had mounted copies of newspaper articles and Quander historical documents to support my claims. I didn't engage the naysayers other than to point out that the historical record spoke for itself.

After the Tricentennial year, it was a relief to not worry about who did not like whom, who was hurting whose feelings, and who was calling whom names. But in March 1985, this temporary quietude with the family was unwittingly disrupted by a call from Fath Ruffins, a Smithsonian historian and consultant, who asked about the feasibility of my preparing a detailed family tree of the Mount Vernon Plantation enslaved and their descendants who were Quander family ancestors. The tree would become part of a forthcoming Smithsonian exhibit, *After the Revolution: Everyday Life in America, 1780–1800*, which would focus on everyday people in the nascent American nation.[1]

As Ruffins explained, while George Washington was not an everyday American, there was a great interest in his enslaved, who themselves led ordinary lives, and their descendants. Based upon President Washington's 1799 inventory of his slaves, plus other historical resources about Washington and his interactions with his slaves, the Smithsonian aimed to dispel myths held by all too many people that family structures and values were alien to and inconsistent with slave life. History reflects that Washington valued family relationships among his enslaved and worked consistently to foster stable relationships in those families, an attribute that was in short supply among many of his fellow slave owners. The family tree of Mount Vernon—descended Quanders would complement the research work of Donald Sweig, Fairfax County historian, who was charting the names and relationships of the Mount Vernon enslaved. The completed exhibit was expected to remain on display for at least a decade.

Fath Ruffins had no idea I had worked day and night to delineate the four main branches of the Quander family tree for the Tricentennial. Although the results were far from complete, I already had something that could be developed into a museum-quality exhibit. In April 1985, I was awarded a contract to conduct research for publication by the Smithsonian Museum of American History. The contract directed that I consult original source materials, including records in Fairfax County in Virginia and Charles and Prince George's Counties in Maryland, and rely upon personal inquiries and other appropriate resources to render a finished product. Although the Smithsonian staff appreciated that the Quander history was significant and stretched back for at least three centuries in America, their immediate interest lay in creating a family tree of Nancy Carter, who married Charles Quander sometime between 1802 and 1810. To get that information, I needed to work with the Mount Vernon Quander descendants, the same Quanders who were the direct descendants of the 1926 QFR founders who had angrily declined to participate in the Tricentennial.

Given the lingering acrimony, did I dare contact them to solicit information, disregarding the warnings of Gladys and others that I was flirting with disaster, inviting myself to be insulted if I reached out to them? Just weeks before, I had determined to leave them alone and let time heal. Now I found myself having to take an obviously angered bull by the horns and wrestle from it vital information for publication by our nation's foremost museum.

After consulting with Gladys and others who were friendly to my efforts, I wrote to key, if hostile, people, explaining exactly what was being requested and why. One of the friendlier Virginia-Pennsylvania Quanders secretly supplied me with a mailing list but admonished me not to tell how I obtained the document. For my follow-up telephone calls, Gladys suggested I not mention the word *Tricentennial* and who was or was not included, as the mere raising of the subject would set certain people off and stop me from gaining the needed information. Lewis Lear Quander suggested making my calls as harmless as possible by asking innocuous questions about the names of ancestors and progeny, plus their dates of birth and death, if deceased. Loretta Carter Hanes wisely pointed out that although my desire was to connect the family's divergent branches, this was not the time to voice that desire.

A few weeks after sending my letter, I began calling younger family members and those I believed would be least hostile. I needed as much information as possible as soon as possible to make progress on the Smithsonian exhibit. Most of them had either received my letter or had been told about it and thus knew what information I needed and understood the significance of the Smithsonian's featuring the Mount Vernon—descended Quanders. Fortunately, most of this first group of people considered it inappropriate to withhold information, regardless of how they felt about me or Quander family connections. But as I expanded my calls to older family members, the responses grew more hostile. Paul Mitchell and Samuel Harmon, both sons of QFR founders, each politely told me that although they had received my letter, they had nothing to say to me. When I explained that all I wanted was to verify some names and dates, they said, "Good day!" and hung up. Other people refused to talk at all, slamming down the telephone with deliberate force. Fortunately, this group was far smaller than I originally feared. But I didn't give up. Most of those who hung up were more receptive to my second call, having mellowed a little after younger family urged them to cooperate but not everyone. Louise Mitchell, Paul Mitchell's sister and matriarch of the North Clan, hung up on me—twice—without uttering a word. I later learned she had requested that no one from the Pennsylvania Quander family speak to me about any aspect of the Smithsonian project. But her sister, Hannah Mitchell Major, despite having been forbidden to talk to me, was helpful, even if reserved. Much earlier than Louise was willing to admit, Hannah agreed there may be a family connection, although when she was growing up, she said, "There was never any mention of a large contingent of Quanders over in DC and Maryland, and none of them ever attend[ed] our reunions in the 1920s and 1930s."

I refrained from pointing out that the Maryland-DC Quanders had not been invited.

Many years later, after the Smithsonian project was hanging on the wall of the Museum of American History, even Louise Mitchell softened, and wrote to my dad that there was a possible, although still unproved, family connection. Before she passed away, I called her in Philadelphia, and although she was firm in her assertion that any family connection remained unconfirmed, we parted on friendly terms, which in itself concluded an important chapter in the Quander family history.

I came to realize that the Smithsonian project was the silver lining I had been searching for. By providing an official answer from a well-regarded external organization to the "What to do?" question, it relieved all of us from deciding who was or was not to be included on family trees and in family reunions. It painted a human side of our family, as well as underscoring my commitment to fostering and preserving the Quander name and place in American history. In November 1985, the multipart exhibit opened as a component of the Smithsonian's permanent display. *After the Revolution: Everyday Life in America, 1780–1800* was a hit from the outset. Two large displays were affixed to the wall in a section primarily devoted to African American life in the post-American Revolutionary War era. One was the family unit structure of George Washington's enslaved, as prepared by Donald Sweig. Immediately next to Sweig's display was the family tree of Charles and Nancy Carter Quander. This exhibit was a fitting and lasting tribute to both of them and a living testimonial to the current generation of Quanders, as the tree included living persons to 1985. Visitors didn't know the turmoil behind the exhibit's Quander family tree, of course, but it proved to us that we could rise above petty differences and work together.

Originally projected to have an eight-to-ten-year-display period, the exhibit's popularity dictated that it remain in place for longer. The display was updated in the mid-1990s, which saw the addition of an extract from a Henry Quando II court case from the 1730s and a table setting of some heirloom china pieces on loan from Loretta Carter Hanes. Beyond the china display, the Smithsonian added a large photograph of Loretta seated at a fully set table of the same china set. The posted narrative explained that she was descended from Rose, Nancy Carter Quander's sister, and that the mostly complete set of china had come from the White House, where an ancestor had worked in the 1920s.

In midsummer 1986, the phone rang again. This time, the caller was from the National Council of Negro Women (NCNW), calling on behalf of Dr. Dorothy I. Height, CEO and national president. Was I available to help Dr. Height publicize NCNW's latest project, "The Black Family Reunion?" The project was an opportunity for African Americans to come together in a public forum to share life experiences, support one another's entrepreneurial efforts, and especially to promote the fostering of strong African American families like the Quander family. The Washington, DC, event was to be the first of many, as the reunion events were to be held in several cities nationwide in 1986 and thereafter annually.

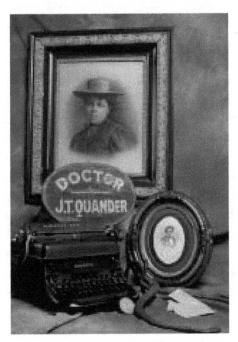

Smithsonian Anacostia Museum Photo advertisement
for *Precious Memories, Collectors Passion* exhibit,
featuring Quander Family, 2002

On a hot afternoon that August, Dr. Height and I met at Howard University's public television station to record "The Black Family Reunion," a thirty-minute program that was used as a planning tool in succeeding years to promote NCNW family reunion events. Dr. Height told me she had been following the Quander family history, especially the Tricentennial Celebration. Our host, Kojo Namdi of *The Evening Exchange*, led the discussion on family values, the roles of mother, father, and children in a family setting, and asked whether there was a secret to having a successful family. We all concluded there was no secret, just several attributes that began and ended with love, but also included caring, compassion, determination, hard work, a measure of discipline, and a commitment to each other. We also agreed that a good sense of values and ethics is needed, something to live by and pass on to the next generation.

The Quanders were also invited by NCNW to lead a panel discussion on the topic "Black Family Conversation" on September 13 and 14, 1986. The Pennsylvania Quanders who saw "The Black Family Reunion" when it aired in Philadelphia expressed pride and satisfaction at the Quanders having been recognized as a strong African American family, worthy of note and an entity to be emulated. When calls were received from Pennsylvania family members inquiring about this event and the upcoming panel discussion, they were invited to join us in Washington for the festivities. As Quanders gathered on the National Mall for a few hours on each of the two days, a few Virginia Quanders who had previously elected to not affiliate were noticeably present. Even more gratifying was the presence of a small band of Pennsylvania Quanders, whose curiosity had surely gotten the best of them. They simply could not stay away, and now in the face of continued national recognition of the family, they concluded it was time to rethink their prior "no family connection" positions. Maybe, just maybe, it was time to let the bygones rest.

We were careful not to ask about their presence. Our tone was one of welcome and inclusiveness. Time was on our side, and we, the upstarts, the dreaded Quanders United, were slowly winning the battle over our being extended family. I could feel an emerging spirit of inclusiveness that seemed to transcend past arguments. Some of the previously hostile family members slowly came to realize that all I ever wanted was to preserve, protect, and share the family's illustrious history. Even so, I continued to stay away from QFR family reunions until 1989. That year's sixty-fourth QFR was held at the Berwyn, Pennsylvania, home of Kenneth and Debbie Mitchell. Ken is a grandson of 1926 QFR founder Georgie Q. Mitchell.

As was traditional, the Saturday afternoon picnic that year was followed by a business meeting before adjourning for the evening. As the meeting was called to order in Ken and Debbie's large family room, a QFR family member stated that Carmen and I, my parents, and a few others were "guests," not QFR members, and he suggested we leave the room while the QFR conducted its business. After a moment of tense silence, Debbie declared that this was her home and we were all family and that no one in the room should leave. Ken immediately agreed with her. "If anyone has anything to say adverse to the Maryland-DC Quanders remaining for the meeting," he said, "please speak up now." No one did. But as I would later learn, the issue was far from forgotten.

Knowing even a small Maryland contingent might cause ripples at a reunion in Pennsylvania, I had already prepared a speech, which I delivered the following day at the Sunday afternoon banquet, that stressed family connections. My focus was upon the central theme for 1989: "We Are Family: The Family of God, the Family of Man, the Family of Quander." Like any tree, I said, we have several roots, branches, and leaves, but just like a tree, one trunk. My message was well received, particularly as I named several ancestors who, by their examples, laid the foundation upon which we have continued to build. Whether farmers, ex-slaves, businesswomen, teachers, laborers, doctors, lawyers, law enforcement, on as leaders in secular and religious organizations, the people who went before us gave us a long-established legacy of contribution and achievements that we are each entitled to tap into and claim as our own. In spite of the tense moments the evening before, when non-QFR members had been asked to leave the room, I came away from the sixty-fourth QFR confident we had vanquished the pervasive doubt that we were one family, no matter how extended we were, and that the sole objective was the preservation and celebration of the Quander family and its many roots and branches. Like Jericho's wall, the wall of division was finally tumbling down.

When there are so many family reunions and events, it is sometimes difficult to recall one in particular. Consequently, I occasionally write a full narrative of a particular occasion, something to pass on to my grandchildren as well as to anyone who might be interested in a specific event. One of these was the sixty-eighth QFR in Norwalk, Connecticut, in August 1993, hosted by Lewis Lear Quander and his lovely wife Eula. Lewis, who at the time was one of the few remaining people who had attended the first QFR in 1926, had for years entreated the family to celebrate a reunion in Connecticut. Numerous private vehicles, plus two charter buses, one each from Virginia and Pennsylvania, all headed for the Holiday Inn, where approximately 125 family members occupied 52 rooms. This particular reunion was special, as it marked the first time that a large group of Maryland-DC Quanders attended the QFR.

Another first took place when a discussion about slavery ensued when I mentioned, during the business meeting after the picnic, that the tenth annual observance of the 1983 construction of the Mount Vernon Slave Memorial would occur the following month. Because of our historical connection to Mount Vernon, the family had been invited by Black Women United for Action and the Mount Vernon Ladies Association to be their honored guests for the planned activities. I was interrupted before I could even finish my announcement.

For many African Americans, the issue of slavery is an ingrained component of American history, and whenever the issue is raised, it can quickly become a festering sore point. To many members of our older generations, in particular, mentioning the subject exposes raw nerves. Some elders recall what Grandma, an old uncle, or some other relative related about how the ancestors were grossly overworked, often suffered brutality, and were even raped at the hand of "old massa." Some Quander elders harbored that same animus, but it was a two-edged sword. On one side, the Mount Vernon—descended Quanders have the putative Washington sanguine connection, which sets them apart from the majority of African Americans. On the other side, simmering resentment remains against the Washington family for subjecting our forebears to involuntary servitude.

That afternoon, the mere mention of the slave memorial anniversary observance sparked an argument. Certain family members railed against George Washington and demanded to know why we should participate in such an event. In their minds, the observance only highlighted the legacy of involuntary servitude. In response, then President Bill Golden attempted to explain the significance of the slave memorial and why it was created. He underscored the value of honoring the unsung ancestors, several of whom were our own family, adding that they deserved our respect and appreciation. To the dissenters, this explanation made no difference, and they continued to interrupt the business meeting. Keeping the meeting on track took a chorus of the majority yelling, "Let's move on! We can't resolve this issue today." There was no final resolution to the issue of our participation in the slave memorial anniversary, and it smoldered for the rest of the weekend.

The sixty-eighth QFR was also marked by another old issue, but this one was germane only to us Quanders. For several years, the QFR executive committee had tried to obtain the original QFR minutes, handwritten for over thirty years by Rose Q. Harmon. Bernard Brooks, great-grandson of QFR Founder Susannah Q. Napper, insisted on keeping the minute book for "safekeeping." When he was still a teenager, Bernard had been asked by older family members to guard the minute book as a means of protecting the family history. Although I was aware of this festering issue, I had no idea of the extent to which Bernard's ongoing refusal to surrender the minutes plagued the QFR leaders and general membership. The matter was discussed, but as no resolution was possible, it was tabled. A few people suggested that court action was appropriate to force Bernard to yield the book. I believed such an approach would only fan the flames, and I did not want to be involved in any action that could lead to an allegation that the Quanders United upstarts were seeking to take over. A few days later, attempting a more personal touch, Gladys talked to Bernard about yielding custody of the book to the QFR. He refused.

Often in life, things get worse before they can get any better. Still furious over having been asked to surrender the minute book and further determined to not concede there might be room for more than one component of the Quander family, in September 1993, Bernard wrote a letter to the Virginia-Pennsylvania groups purporting to clarify matters. He asserted that he wrote solely for dealing with a matter of utmost urgency and on behalf of the descendants of those who were present at the first QFR on August 15, 1926. But by listing who was present at that reunion, Bernard exposed an old but sensitive nerve. His itemized list named not a single descendant of dairy farmer Charles Henry Quander, whose descendants, you might recall, were not invited to the QFR until 1930. As 1994 dawned, what had been intended to pull several of the Virginia Quanders away from their Maryland-DC counterparts had the opposite effect. The letter inadvertently underscored that there was no room for divisiveness, as we needed to look ahead toward the preservation and expansion of the reunion and not backward to limit it to the Mount-Vernon-connected descendants of the first reunion.

The consensus in Virginia was that dwelling on past hurts that excluded many of the Virginia Quanders from the QFR until 1930 would only keep all of us in a negative frame of mind and accomplish nothing. Bernard's effort was marginalized, but that did not stop him and a small group of followers from planning a separate reunion in 1994, the tenth anniversary of the Tricentennial Celebration at Howard University. Quanders United and QFR planned to hold a joint reunion in Virginia that year with the theme, "The Tricentennial plus Ten Quander Family Reunion, 1684–1994."

What a weekend that was! With more than 250 people present, thanks to the skillful efforts of the planning committee, our program was a great success. Quanders United sponsored the Asante Kotoko Association of Ghana whose members, clothed in traditional dress, poured libation, and—in more than one Ghanaian language—entreated the favorable presence and blessing of the ancestors. Using their talking drums for rhythm, they also demonstrated traditional Ghanaian dancing and recruited several of us to join in, feel the spirit, and learn about the dance culture of our Amkwandoh ancestors. We also had a historic photograph slide presentation, an African fashion show, a grand picnic on Saturday afternoon, a swimming pool party at the hotel's covered pavilion, and—of course—church on Sunday followed by dinner and a program at the Howard Johnson.

Meanwhile, about twenty-five people had trickled in to the Days Inn down the road to celebrate what was labeled the "Original Quander Family Reunion." They quickly realized that efforts to set things straight had largely failed, as family members from all sectors were committed to the success of joint efforts. Several of the Days Inn group would later state they did not know there were two separate reunions that weekend, just one mile apart on the Jefferson Davis Highway, but with a world of difference. Although they had paid their money to the other event and participated in some of its activities, they still found time to fraternize with us. At midnight Friday, I found myself in the Howard Johnson restaurant with several members of the family who were lamenting their participation in the "Original Quander Family Reunion." They vowed to bring a swift end to divisiveness and the misunderstandings and miscommunications of the past. As I heard more than once that night, "The Quander family reunions are my birthright, something that I have done all my life, and I don't plan to give them up now. There can't be two reunions. This will never happen again."

Breakfast Saturday morning was at Gladys's home on Hampton Road, just off Quander Road. Gladys related that the peaches and grapes used to make her homemade jellies were picked by the staff of Mount Vernon, grown on trees and vines descended from plants which, the staff proudly proclaimed, were planted and grown by George Washington himself. With Gladys leading the way, several of us commented that it was far more accurate to say the trees and vines were planted by our Quander ancestors and their fellow enslaved. We do not fool ourselves. We believe the story should be truthful in the telling.

The annual reunion picnic, with about 150 people in attendance, was close to perfect. Threatened rain never materialized, and clouds gave way to sun by early afternoon. The highlight of the day was Guy Mitchell's freshly caught rainbow trout, spots, and perch, which were absolutely scrumptious. We learned that evening that the other picnic had degenerated into a raucous, argumentative affair, with William Golden, past president of the QFR, North Clan, challenging the propriety of holding a separate, much smaller reunion. It was reported that the picnic's atmosphere was so foul that several of the few attendees, principally from Pennsylvania, left before the planned ending time. At our pool party, one of the defectors exclaimed, "Even the food was nasty!" a verification of the common belief that a bad attitude can spoil everything.

It was difficult for many family members, young and old, to understand why other family members could act so badly toward one another. Many of the younger people spent much of the celebratory weekend discussing the issue, and I was asked several times by younger relatives why some of us elected to go elsewhere rather than be a part of the Tricentennial plus Ten. There was no single or simple answer that satisfied their curiosity and dismay.

When we convened the next year in Mount Laurel, New Jersey, just outside of Philadelphia, there was an air of anticipation, a feeling there was no issue we could not solve working as a unit. Most immediately apparent was the absence of anyone who could be considered a dissenter. The acrimonious days of the recent past had subsided, replaced with a new and much more appreciated spirit of cooperation. Almost all the holdout descendants came to realize that to keep the QFR torch burning required an infusion of other Quanders. The QFR is stable for now. But as we progress toward the one hundredth anniversary of the QFR in 2026, the efforts required to keep the reunion functioning and us together as a family impose new and greater challenges. I sincerely hope that as we approach 2026 and beyond that the two mottos—"Blest Be the Ties That Bind" from the Virginia-Pennsylvania Quanders and "We Are Many, but We Are One" from the Maryland—Washington, DC, Quanders—will not be empty words but will guide our personal and family beliefs and serve as the incentives needed to hold us together.

CHAPTER 11

◆◆◆◆◆

The Mount Vernon Slave Memorial

Gladys Quander Tancil, whose ancestors were enslaved for decades at George Washington's Mount Vernon estate, was the first and, for many years, the only African American tour guide at Mount Vernon. When she quietly pointed out that Saturday morning at the sixty-ninth QFR that President Washington himself had not planted the forebears of the peach trees and grapevines from which our breakfast jellies came, she knew what she was talking about. But her position at Mount Vernon was a long time in coming.

The Mount Vernon Ladies Association (MVLA), formed in 1853, has owned Mount Vernon and everything at the site since 1858.[1] Their mission includes maintaining the Mount Vernon mansion and estate and promoting George Washington's legacy as the "father of our country."[2] In 1929, the MVLA placed a flat two-by-four-foot white marble marker at the estate's all-but-forgotten slave burial ground. No ceremony marked the placement of the marble slab. The burial ground remained untended, and the marker was soon lost in the weeds. Few people remembered the unmarked graves.

What prompted the MVLA to lay the marker? The documentation from the 1928 MVLA meeting minutes, when the marker was being discussed and voted on, is sparse.[3] The first entry notes that a Mrs. Maxey "requested a simple marker be placed on the ground which was used by General and Mrs. Washington for the burial of slaves." The next entry, from the Tomb Committee, is more expansive:

"The graveyard which was used by General and Mrs. Washington for his slaves is unmarked. In the course of time it is possible all traces of the graves will disappear. It is recommended that a simple marker, suitably inscribed, be placed on this consecrated ground." Later, minutes from 1928 comment that the marker should be of stone, something permanent, and ask permission from the MVLA governing body to suitably mark the burial place. The story picks up the following year. We learn from the MVLA *Minutes* entry of March 16, 1929, that Artie Pettit and Austin Pettit (relationship unknown) began digging the base area upon which the tablet marker would lie, and on March 28, 1929, the "ledger monument" was delivered to Mount Vernon and installed the same day. The cost of the Georgian marble marker was $135. The next and final entry for the period is dated May 1929:

> After fruitless efforts to find any account of interments of Mount Vernon servants, the ancient burial site—on the ridge southwest of the Tomb—is now permanently marked by a memorial stone supplied by a very kind and generous lady. The epitaph read: "In Memory of the Many Faithful Colored Servants of the Washington Family, Buried at Mount Vernon from 1760–1860. Their Unidentified Graves Surround This Spot."

Entries in the *Minutes* regarding the burial site go silent until December 6, 1947, when a visit to the site by "WB" and "IW" is noted. The two visitors were interviewed by Mr. Freeman, a park policeman. The comments stated, "WB and IW noted a presence of twenty-five to thirty graves, including one still standing tombstone, that of Nathan Johnson, dated 1885. Mr. Bailey [probably WB] stepped down into a hole, probably about two feet deep." On December 17, 1947, a follow-up entry refers to a conversation from twenty years before: "Artie Pettit placed the tablet and, during that time, had a conversation with a George Ford, who then worked at

Mount Vernon. Ford told Pettit that he was born on the property and that both his parents were buried at the site.[4] Ford also noted that there was a colored man, Mr. Quanders, who had worked here but is now blind." The "colored man" was Tom Quander, longtime gardener and landscaper at Mount Vernon.

For years, although I had visited Mount Vernon countless times, I had no clue where the enslaved had been buried. None of the tour guides ever mentioned the slave burial ground on the many tours I had taken with out-of-town relatives and friends who wanted to see where George Washington lived. This conspiracy of silence characterized how most people seemed to feel. We all knew Mount Vernon had been maintained by enslaved people, but no one wanted to talk about it. Whites were too sensitive to bring it up in any but the most discreet conversations and even then generally referred to the slaves using the MVLA's euphemism, "servants." And African Americans were also loath to mention it, partly still seething in anger, partly in embarrassment and a continuing sense of humiliation for how our ancestors were treated.

The burial ground of Washington's enslaved remained largely unseen until 1982 when student discussion in a research class taught by Dr. Lillian D. Anthony at George Mason University turned to family and oral histories. Some of the students' ancestors had been enslaved in Northern Virginia, and the questions they asked and issues they raised that day ultimately led to the creation of the Slave Memorial at Mount Vernon.

Dr. Anthony obtained a research grant through the Black Studies Department at George Mason University to film a documentary on the historic and contemporary Black presence in Fairfax County. A major part of her time was spent at Mount Vernon, inquiring about slave life and the contributions of the long-dead Mount Vernon enslaved to the operation of the estate. Arriving with the rest of her team (the documentary director, a still photographer, and a video cameraman) on a bitterly cold day, she learned from an African American employee at the entrance gate of Mount Vernon that over yonder—he pointed toward the road that leads to the Washington mausoleum—there is also a slave graveyard. This was the first time

Anthony realized that the Washington enslaved were buried at the site in significant numbers. The ground was covered in four inches of freshly fallen snow. "[We saw] only rusted barbed wire and heavy overgrowth with no visible objects and a few trees," she later wrote. "It was so cold that the video camera froze, [but] luckily, we had our still camera. We began to canvas the area, kicking the underbrush as we went. My foot hit something so hard, my foot was in pain."[5] Anthony had found the MVLA's flat, white marble marker the hard way.

The interment ground of the slave ancestors is located only twenty-five yards southwest from where George Washington and his family are buried, yet it is a world away. The men and women who literally slaved at Mount Vernon for decades were placed in pine coffins in unmarked graves. Washington was interred in a marble sarcophagus housed above ground within an open-front red brick mausoleum carved with symbols and words that extol the accomplishments of Washington and his family. When Anthony and her team located the burial ground that cold winter day, there were no paths, signs, or brochures that gave the slightest hint of its presence. They cleaned the snow off the marker with their hands so it could be photographed. As Anthony looked at the marble marker, her thoughts drifted to another time when hundreds of Washington slaves had toiled for decades, unknown, unappreciated, and unable to taste the freedoms and rights of citizenship. More than sympathy, she felt an appreciation that these dead were a determined lot, who died in faith and hope for a better time, although most of them never lived to enjoy those freedoms. Tears welled up in her eyes, and then she got angry.

Anthony resolved to make a difference. Part of her effort to have the burial ground properly recognized resulted in a brief but hard-hitting February 1982 *Washington Post* article by Dorothy Gilliam that criticized the site's obvious lack of care and visibility as well as an interpretation of how the interred had been a vital part of George Washington's estate.[6] Motivated by Gilliam's cogent call to action, several local residents rallied for the creation of an appropriate lasting honor for the contributions of the Mount Vernon enslaved. MVLA immediately consented to the memorial request.

Several planning meetings were held in 1982 to determine what type of memorial should be constructed and by whom.[7] A design contest among Howard University architectural students elicited more than a dozen entries. The winning design was a gray granite column constructed at the center of three concentric granite circles. The top of the column, cut at an angle, bears the inscription, "In memory of the Afro Americans who served as slaves at Mount Vernon." FAITH, HOPE, and LOVE—the virtues that sustained the people who lived in bondage under George Washington—are inscribed on the edge of the circular platform upon which the marker rests. Boxwoods grow in the inner circle around the column, the young plants being harvested from mature plants grown at Mount Vernon by the ancestral slaves themselves. Ground was broken on February 21, 1983, for the awe-inspiring memorial, which was dedicated on September 21, just seven months from the ground breaking.

Several dignitaries attended the dedication, including Governor Charles S. Robb, who noted that the dedication of the Slave Memorial was a posthumous completion of the passage into full human dignity that Washington had envisioned in the emancipation of the men and women whose station as slaves Washington came to see was fundamentally incompatible with the American freedom that he had helped bring into being. He reminded the audience that the history of America must be the history of all Americans and that the memorial was a repayment of an immeasurable and long unacknowledged debt.[8] With the dedication of the Slave Memorial came a new set of printed materials about Mount Vernon, more focused upon the presence and contributions of the enslaved. There were many discussions among the MVLA, the Mount Vernon library staff, and African American contributors regarding what to say about the enslaved, slavery, and George Washington's role as a slaveholder. However, much of what was suggested for inclusion in the printed brochure was not adopted, due to the inability to prove certain assertions and the continued sensitivity over the issue of slavery.

After the hoopla surrounding the dedication of the Slave Memorial in 1983, for the following seven years, little occurred to promote any awareness of its existence. There was no organized effort to tell visitors about the people to whom the memorial was dedicated and the meaningful and crucial roles they played in the successful operation of Mount Vernon. The MVLA was uneasy about how to proceed, especially as they have a stodgy image among African Americans, many of whom still harbor resentment against George Washington for his role as one of Virginia's largest slaveholders. African Americans well recall that Washington elected to free his enslaved only upon his death, even providing in his will for the postponement of their manumission until after his wife's death. Often, they have repeated that the true measure of his greatness would have been taking the bold step of manumitting his enslaved during his lifetime, which would have set the tone for fulfilling the promises of liberty and equality to all persons on American soil. To some observers, any promotion of the Slave Memorial by the MVLA might have been viewed as extolling a presumed virtue in the slavery that existed at Mount Vernon throughout most of its history. In 1990, Black Women United for Action (BWUFA) stepped into this void. BWUFA members, who were determined to raise local and national awareness of the Slave Memorial, began with a rededication of the memorial that included the first annual wreath-laying ceremony on September 22, 1990. In his keynote address, Governor L. Douglas Wilder, the first African American elected as governor of a state since Reconstruction, gave voice to what had long been ignored: "More than a few plantation owners achieved the American dream at the price of the African American nightmare."

Although hundreds—perhaps even thousands—of buildings, parks, statues, and other memorials are dedicated to the Confederacy and the men who served it, the greater portion of whom were most likely enslavers, in 1990, there were no other permanent tribute memorials in the United States dedicated to those African Americans who were pressed into slavery. Appreciating that slave contributions were at the heart of building this nation and that African Americans continue to contribute to the American Dream on all levels, BWUFA determined to ensure that a national focus be continuously placed upon the Slave Memorial and the contributions made by the African American men, women, and children who slaved to build this nation.

Every year since 1990, BWUFA and MVLA have cosponsored the annual Slave Memorial wreath-laying ceremony. The yearly program format is a memorial service designed to remind everyone who these people were, what they did, and that they died in faith that a better day was coming, if not for them, then at least for their children. BWUFA's statement for the Tenth Anniversary Slave Memorial Wreath-Laying Ceremony, held on September 18, 1993, noted that this "event is not about slavery or laying a wreath at a memorial, it is about acknowledging the strength of a noble and forgotten people who contributed greatly to the prosperity and formation of this nation." The annual program has expanded its mission in recent years to include recognizing modern day slavery and saluting the antislavery organizations dedicated to the eradication of human trafficking.

Since the Slave Memorial was dedicated in 1983 and particularly since its rededication in 1990, there has been a marked increase in visitation at Mount Vernon by African Americans. The focus is not so much upon paying any tribute to George Washington as it is the realization of a shared common history of the unsung—that is, of their having worked long, hard, and usually without any recognition to make Washington look his very best. This practice was common and accepted at estates like Thomas Jefferson's Monticello and the other great plantations operated by the Southern gentlemen farmers who framed the Declaration of Independence, the Constitution, and the Bill of Rights.

I remember as a child, teenager, and young adult coming to Mount Vernon on many occasions. The tour guides would drone on and on about George Washington and what a great man he was. They would talk about his noble deeds, his inability to tell a lie, and even refer to the cherry tree he allegedly cut down when he was young. Only a passing reference was made to the people who served him, and even then, they were euphemistically called "servants." The words *slave*, *slavery*, and *slave owner* were never uttered, and when more than one tourist questioned why not, the sheepish reply was most often, "The Washingtons referred to their help as servants, so we use the same term." That slip-slide response failed to elude the hard question and embittered many who dared to ask the obvious.

Not surprisingly, inadequate answers of this type contributed to the low attendance by African Americans at Mount Vernon.

But gradually, I noticed a more open attitude, still with some reticence, but a loosening up among the staff. Quietly, the word *servant* was replaced with *slave*. Certainly, this change was due to some personnel coming to the realization that as a man of his times, George Washington shared attitudes and viewpoints typical of his day, and that the continued glorification of him as flawless and larger than life was stirring up dissension, especially within the African American community.

By the early 1970s, Mount Vernon acknowledged the need to rectify the lack of African American tour guides working at the site. Periodic newspaper advertisements never met with success, as African Americans continued to resent Washington for not freeing his slaves until he died. The all-White tour guide situation changed one day in 1975, when Gladys, who had been in occasional part-time domestic service at Mount Vernon for twelve years, called the main kitchen to ask a question about the Washington family's dietary preferences. She was directed to Christine Meadows, one of the Mount Vernon curators. As the conversation ensued and discussions about the history of Mount Vernon continued, Meadows asked Gladys if she would like to work as a "historical interpreter," the term Mount Vernon then used for its tour guides. Gladys was interested, and with her distinguished and long-term historical connection to Mount Vernon on both sides of her Quander-Carter family and a strong penchant for history, she was hired on the spot.

Gladys was the only nonwhite tour guide for the greater part of twenty years. Her presence did not necessarily increase the number of African Americans visiting Mount Vernon, but once they saw this gray-haired, knowledgeable tour guide, they were drawn to her. Regularly, they asked her questions about slave life at the plantation that Gladys believed they would not have asked the White tour guides. Typical queries were, "Are you a descendant from any of the Mount Vernon slaves?" to which Gladys answered that Nancy Carter Quander, a collateral ancestor, was a Mount Vernon slave, as were some of her other ancestors.[9] Also, "As a Black person, what is your attitude toward George Washington as a slave owner?" Her most typical reply was that slavery was a horrible institution Washington at first willingly and later reluctantly supported. He freed his enslaved eventually. But it was still slavery, and we can't forget that, she'd say. All in all, he was a great man nevertheless. Eventually, White visitors began asking her race-and-slavery-related questions, including questions about interracial sexual activity, all part of what I have noted was a heightened curiosity and changed attitude about the institution of slavery.

In spite of MVLA's recognition that slavery was a severe blemish upon not only George Washington but America as well, Gladys was cautioned in her early training to downplay the institution of slavery at Mount Vernon and not to mention the enslaved burial ground. If visitors specifically inquired, she was to answer as briefly as possible, and she was to direct them to the then undeveloped burial ground only if they asked to be so directed. But over time, the Slave Memorial rapidly became a main attraction at Mount Vernon, and by the 1990s, the MVLA recognized the need to include slavery as an integral component of Mount Vernon's history and legacy. For reluctant MVLA members, the issue was how to tell the slave story while protecting George Washington's legacy. Increasingly, the Mount Vernon staff and other experts beyond the plantation's boundaries were conducting expanded research of the site, uncovering details of slave life at Mount Vernon and in the old South in general. From that research and the expanded interest in slavery among its visitors and partly to meet the competition from Williamsburg and Monticello, in April 1995, MVLA initiated something previously unthinkable: the Slave Life Tour.

The new tour would incorporate the operation of the Mount Vernon plantation from the perspective of the enslaved. Just how did this huge place run? What types of knowledge and skills were required to be a cook, blacksmith, cooper, carpenter, gardener, painter, brick maker, coachman, boatman, fisherman, spinner, weaver, seamstress—to name a few occupations—at this essentially self-contained plantation? It is widely recognized that Mount Vernon was run as an efficient operation particularly because of the skills of the slave labor force that resided there—the men, women, and children who performed the day-to-day chores and carried on whether or not General Washington was in residence. Washington had a Revolutionary War to fight and later a nation to run. He could never have achieved the level of success and public recognition he enjoyed if the home front was not being managed well or if the skills and expert knowledge of the people he owned were wanting in any significant way. It is believed that fully one-third of the enslaved was skilled in a trade or had a craft while another large segment was experienced in the sometimes unpredictable art of farming.

Gladys Quander Tancil (1921-2002),
first African American Interpreter Guide at Mount Vernon

By 1995, Gladys had already been serving as an historical interpreter for twenty years. She was tapped to conduct the first Slave Life Tours, and her delivery was widely praised for her candor and insight. Some of the staff were still visibly nervous about raising the issue of slavery at Mount Vernon, especially in the context of Washington as an enslaver. From the outset, Gladys made clear that she would neither sugarcoat the institution of slavery nor castigate Washington as a slave owner. Still she believed slavery was such an integral and undeniable component of Mount Vernon's history that she could not simply whitewash the subject. Gladys told me that the Slave Life Tour allowed her to focus upon the many contributions the enslaved made in operating Mount Vernon rather than continue with the artificial emphasis on George Washington that unrealistically downplayed their enforced contributions over the decades he owned the plantation.

The Slave Life Tour gained in popularity after it was featured in the August 1995 *City Paper* article "Mount Vernon's Other Legacy." The typical Mount Vernon tour focused on the official story that Americans and the world always hear: George and Martha sitting on the portico enjoying the evening breezes from the Potomac River, strolling through their well-endowed gardens, entertaining the rich and powerful of the day, and philosophizing about the new and noble American democracy. In contrast, Gladys took her visitors, about equal numbers of Blacks and Whites, through the less swank portions of the estate.[10] She told them that the Washington slaves lived no differently from most slaves on other Southern plantations, adding, "People really aren't aware of how the slaves suffered, even on the Washington estate." They were exposed to harsh conditions, cramped public living quarters, and the overseer's occasional whip or other forms of punishment. They toiled long hours in dank, dark places and in all types of weather and were bought and sold like animals. She noted that within the enslaved community, there was always some measure of resistance, both to the institution and to the harshness of their condition. Although Washington generally strove not to break up families, which was a redeeming element about him, Gladys would tell her visitors, he still has to be held accountable for owning human beings throughout his adult life. During Washington's ownership of the Mount Vernon plantation, he held more than six hundred people in bondage.

Billie McSeveney, Gladys's supervisor, told the *City Paper* that her tours were extremely successful: "As a descendant, Gladys has a marvelous sense of continuity and a great sense of dignity that she brings to the tour. People who regularly bring groups to Mount Vernon specifically request Gladys to give them the Slave Tour."

The Quander family has continued its active affiliation with Mount Vernon and the Slave Memorial. The MVLA and Mount Vernon staff have long recognized the Quander-Mount Vernon connections from at least three ancestors (Nancy Carter Quander, West Ford, and Tobias Lear), so it is understandable that the family's connection to the first, First Family would be of sustained interest. Several years prior to Gladys's death in 2002 and still continuing today, calls from Mount Vernon for Quander family participation are routine. In June 1996, for example, the Olympic Torch, which was en route to the Summer Games in Atlanta, passed through Mount Vernon. I was asked if I would like to carry the torch when it came to Mount Vernon to represent the African American legacy that is an integral part of the estate's history. Although I was flattered by the request, I suggested that perhaps a younger representative should be selected. Sekila Mali Holmes, Gladys's granddaughter, was chosen to serve as the torchbearer and represent not only the Quander and Carter families but also all the forgotten people of Mount Vernon and their descendants.

A year later, in September 1997, I received a telephone call from Sheila Coates, president of BWUFA. It was Monday evening. Could I be at Mount Vernon Thursday morning, when President Bill Clinton was scheduled to place a wreath on the Slave Memorial? Gladys was also invited, and we were both delighted at the prospect. On Wednesday, the venue was moved from Mount Vernon to the White House allegedly because heavy rain was predicted and the president's schedule was tight. Still there was a subtext feeling that President Clinton's presence at the actual memorial site might be misinterpreted as an apology for slavery, a political position that at the time many thought should not be suggested.

The following morning in the Executive Office Building, immediately after the formal speeches, an aide came to where Gladys and I and other Mount Vernon people were sitting and asked us to accompany her. We walked out of the Executive Office Building, across a courtyard, and through the western side entrance of the White House. This was the first time I had ever been in this part of the White House, as all my prior visits were strictly the standard fare offered to tourists. Eventually, we found ourselves just outside the Oval Office. The door swung open, and there stood President Bill Clinton, Vice President Al Gore, and Senator Charles Robb of Virginia. Immediately, President Clinton stepped forward to shake our hands and warmly welcome us to the Oval Office.

President William J. Clinton, with Gladys Quander
Tancil, Rohulamin Quander, and Senator Charles Robb
in the White House Oval Office, September 1997

President William J. Clinton, with a group, including
Gladys Quander Tancil and Rohulamin Quander in
the White House Oval Office, September 1997

As we all stood there feeling a little overwhelmed, Sheila Coates said to the president, indicating Gladys and me, "These are members of the Quander family, who were slaves to President Washington." I was standing next to President Clinton, absorbing the magnificence of the room, when he wrapped his left arm over my shoulder. I was electrified by that simple act, which he complemented by looking me straight in the eye, a characteristic for which he is well noted. He said, "We're pleased to have you here."

The White House photographer asked everyone to take a position for the official photograph. As she finalized the pose, she said, "Let's put this beautiful lady between you two," and directed Gladys to stand between me and the president. I kept thinking, *This photo will surely be on the cover of my book on the family, as the historical significance of the moment must be conveyed for future Quander generations.* How I wish Henry Quando and his family and all his descendants could have seen Gladys and me in the Oval Office with the president of the United States! Coates then presented President

Clinton with a replica of the Slave Memorial, and it was all over as quickly as it had begun.

But not quite over. After waiting about three weeks for my copy of the photograph with the president, I inquired of BWUFA and was told to be patient. Four weeks, six weeks, eight weeks passed. Just how patient was I supposed to be? After about twelve weeks, Sheila Coates told me that the issue of releasing the photographs had become politically sensitive because President Clinton's posing with us and his receiving the replica of the Slave Memorial could be interpreted as his making an apology for slavery. The White House simply would not release the photographs. A conference call to the White House liaison officer who helped set up the photo session was less than enlightening, resulting only in a stern denial that the photographs were being held hostage, tendering rather that they appeared to be "lost."

I began to wonder if the photograph's curious disappearance was the result of a political decision. With the Commission on Race Relations in America having been established by President Clinton that year (1997) to study the state of race relations, including America's troubled racial past, which intertwines with all aspects of life in America, the thought that a mere photograph of Gladys and me with President Clinton in the Oval Office could be interpreted as an apology for slavery seriously boggled my mind. But only days later, several newspapers reported that the president was scheduled to meet with national-level conservatives who urged him to make no apology for America's slaveholding past, no matter what the commission's report and recommendations contained. So I remained of the opinion that maybe the failure to release the photos of our visit to the Oval Office was related to this anti-apology stance.

In all, this story has a happy ending. The photograph was belatedly located, having allegedly been shipped out of the White House with some other photographs, and then misplaced for a considerable amount of time before Gladys and I finally received our copies.

Quander family members have continued to participate in Mount Vernon events into the twenty-first century, including being photographed for the annual press release announcing the Slave Memorial ceremony and delivering remarks for the occasion; laying the boxwood wreath on the memorial after the tribute program in the grove; dedicating the slave cabin replica on the lower land; planting a memorial tree using soil taken from the five original farm sites of the Mount Vernon estate; and rededicating the brick slave dormitory after a major restoration. One of the most moving activities for me was serving as a consultant to the Mount Vernon exhibit *Lives Bound Together: Slavery at George Washington's Mount Vernon*, which opened in October 2016.[11] Unlike almost every other slave-related exhibit in America, this one focused upon the lives of the enslaved themselves, with enslaver George Washington relegated to the periphery of the interpretation. The exhibit was scheduled to remain until September 2020.

Entrance to slavery exhibit at Mount Vernon, *Lives Bound Together, Slavery at George Washington's Mount Vernon*

156

In preparation for *Lives Bound Together*, in 2014, a team of archaeologists, using the most updated digital techniques available, conducted soil anomaly studies in the enslaved burial ground to locate as many grave sites as possible. Remote sensing of the site in the early 1980s confirmed at least seventy-five grave-shaped soil anomalies oriented on an east-west axis, suggesting that the heads of the interred pointed toward Africa or perhaps toward the rising sun. The 2014 study suggested there are significantly more burials at the site, possibly as many as 150. Nothing is known of these people. They lie nameless in their unmarked graves.

Rohulamin and Carmen Torruella
Quander at Mount Vernon, c2012

Although I served as a consultant to *Lives Bound Together*, none of the Quander family's written historical records that I have uncovered mention any Quanders who are buried at Mount Vernon. For decades, family has simply referred to "the Mount Vernon connection," which to us means that Quanders and Quander-related families slaved at Mount Vernon, some dying there, and now presumably buried in the designated slave burial ground. The most obvious is

West Ford, whose granddaughter Hannah Bruce Ford married John Pierson Quander in about 1868. He was a direct descendant from Charles and Nancy Carter Quander. Other likely burial candidates—all whom were Washington's enslaved—are Sukey Bay, Nancy Carter Quander's mother, who is noted in the early 1830s as still under the care of the Washington estate, and referred to in certain documents as old, blind, and in need of nursing care; Nancy Carter Quander, Sukey Bay's daughter and possibly her freeborn husband, Charles Quander; Rose, Nancy's sister and Sukey Bay's daughter; several members of the Carter family who married into the Quander family too many times to enumerate here; and William Hayes, a former Washington enslaved and Nancy Quander's son-in-law, who was married to Elizabeth Quander Hayes and who, along with Nancy, was listed among the ten men and one woman in a November 16, 1835, article in the *Alexandria Gazette* that identified them as tending Washington's grave.

Quanders gather at slave cabin reproduction
at Mount Vernon during the 85th annual
Quander Family reunion, 2010

In August 2010, the Quander family gathered at Mount Vernon to celebrate our eighty-fifth annual QFR. It was a joyous occasion that featured a boat ride on the Potomac, a tour of the entire estate, and lunch for 150 family members and a few guests. Members of the press were present in significant numbers. Over the course of the weekend celebration, National Public Radio featured me on "Talk of the Nation," and CNN did a program that was seen nationally by millions of viewers. The *Washington Post* and the *Afro American* did photo features on the family's historical connection to Mount Vernon for that reunion event.

Quanders gather at Mount Vernon Slave
Memorial in tribute to interred ancestors
during 85th annual reunion, 2010

As the luncheon's keynote speaker, I asked the assemblage to think about the time of our ancestors' servitude and then ask themselves, "What hope did any of them have?" Nothing was promised. Most of us from that era knew little about what lay beyond Mount Vernon. Surely, this circumstance created some of the greatest personal frustrations known to women or men, as reflected in the thoughtful words of our cousin, Lewis Lear Quander, in his poem, "Miracle of Faith: Tribute to My Mount Vernon Ancestors." Reflecting on the decades that passed before slavery was even mentioned at Mount Vernon, I reminded my family, "None of us should be embarrassed about our ancestry that includes enslavement, and indeed, that condition is an important element in the formation of the strengths and determinations about who we are, will become, and what we represent today."

An interviewer asked, as visitors used to ask Gladys, "How do the Quanders feel today about the fact that George Washington permanently enslaved several of your ancestors, denying them even the rudiments of education?" Our response was largely universal. As Quanders, we cannot view Washington in only one dimension. Family members answered much as Gladys had, noting that Washington was a man of his time, but still holding him accountable for upholding the evils of human bondage. Many acknowledged his major step in setting an example and freeing those who involuntarily served him, although not until his own death. Although George Washington's image must be protected, we would do ourselves and all Mount Vernon visitors a great disservice if we failed to accurately describe the harshness that characterized servitude at Mount Vernon and elsewhere.

As a licensed tour guide in Washington, DC, I escort students and others to Mount Vernon several times per year. The various reactions to visiting a former slaveholding plantation, including comments that slavery was not really all that bad an institution, never cease to amaze me. I emphasize and this is particularly important for young people to understand that the historical significance is not so much that there is a Quander connection to the Washington family, as it is the importance of placing everything in its proper perspective. I tell my tour participants that the history of slavery is a very dark mark on the history of the United States and that we have to confront that history and face its related issues head-on if we are ever going have a better understanding of and cooperation between all the racial and ethnic groups that make up the United States. Only then will true racial harmony become the order of the day.

Yes, there is a strong Quander-Washington-Mount Vernon connection. Let that connection be a beacon about what happened and how, why, and when it happened. But let it also light the way to a better future when we, as Americans all, can realize more fully who we are and where we came from. And indeed, there is more to where Quanders came from than seventeenth-century American plantations. Like other African Americans, we trace our heritage to Africa.

CHAPTER 12

Coming Full Circle
A Trip to Ghana

There was no question in my mind at the conclusion of the 1984 Tricentennial Celebration, especially after our research to establish the Quander family coat of arms, that our history would remain incomplete as long as we neglected our African connection. Earlier that year, when Ernest Kweku Amaquandoh and his brother Joseph Kojo Amaquandoh visited from New York, they introduced us to the ancestral spelling "Amkwandoh," which was the standard spelling from the nineteenth century, until the British anglicized "Kw" to "Qu." The Amaquandoh brothers also told us of the ancestral village of Kankaboom, in Ghana's Cape Coast region, where many of the residents were Amaquandohs. When their father, Joseph Egyir (Ebenezer) Amaquandoh, learned of the American Quanders, he had spurred them to tell us the story of Egya Edoum Amkwandoh, the son of Apprendontwe Amkwandoh, who was a prominent general.

Egya, who at birth was recognized by the native priests as a special child, was ordained as one who would be a protector of his people in future generations. From childhood, he was respected, even venerated, and grew to be a good and spiritual young man. His followers wanted him to organize a resistance to the slave trade, using military means, if necessary, when he was a little older. By his late teens, Egya had already organized some resistance efforts. But earning a living was still necessary. One day, Egya, one of his brothers, their sister Niarko, and several other villagers headed out from the adjacent villages of Kankaboom and Episidasi. They intended to go to the coast to barter palm oil or perhaps, as another version of the story indicated, palm wine. They never made it. The group was set upon by slave catchers, and Egya was captured. Niarko and her brother ran back to the village to report this disaster and hastily organize a search party, but after looking for months, they gave up. Egya was never seen again. They concluded he had been taken to one of the area slave castles—actually jails—and would soon be put onto a slave ship bound for the Americas and delivered to a harsh and brutal life of permanent enslavement.

To my query to Kojo about how often this type of incident occurred, he replied, "Not very often because the ancestors lived close to the coast and the slave catchers generally preferred to go into the interior for their slaves. They often cultivated relationships with the coastal people, as they did not want their rear flanks to be hostile." Kojo added that the village elders did not know of any other Amkwandohs, except for Egya, who were captured and taken away. I found that claim difficult to accept, despite the inclination of the slave catchers wanting to keep peace with the people who resided along the coastal areas, while they proceeded further into the interior. But this practice raised an interesting question.

"Did these seventeenth-century Amkwandohs cooperate with or assist the slave catchers?" I asked. Kojo was a bit insulted by my question but admitted he could not answer, as none of the elders even hinted at cooperation with the enslavers. "However," he added, "some of the coastal people, aided by other Africans from the area, helped build the slave castles that ringed the coastal areas and housed the newly captured slaves." I realized Kojo was unwittingly admitting that a certain level of complicity existed, with the coastal Africans rendering valuable services that enabled the enslavers to carry out their cruel and inhumane deeds. But because the coastal people and the Amkwandohs in particular did not generally suffer enslavement, Kojo's father and the other elders of the Amaquandoh clan firmly believed Egya's capture was unique and that therefore he was the forebear of the entire American Quander family.

The story of Egya Edoum left me with many questions and few answers. I realized a trip to Ghana was necessary. Not that such a trip would answer all my many questions, but it would be of great significance for the American Quanders to establish personal and direct contact with their likely Ghanaian counterparts, the Amaquandohs.[1]

With a burning desire to learn more but unwilling to chance the grueling trip himself because of his lifelong diabetes, my father resolved that Carmen and I would be his representatives. I laid my plans for the trip, promoted as a triumphant return of the progeny of Egya Edoum Amkwandoh to the ancestral homeland and village. We left Washington on July 21, 1991. Carmen and I had purchased large quantities of items to barter for indigenous Ghanaian products, as well as gifts for Amaquandohs whom we were yet to meet, and we had far more baggage than we normally would have. An obliging Trans World Airlines employee who recognized me from television appearances relating to the Quander family history helped move us through the ticket line, the baggage check-in, and the metal detectors.

Our departure from Washington National Airport to London was delayed a full hour. This delay and waiting in the close air of the parked jet turned out to be part of our orientation to life in Ghana, where waiting and being late were traditional. From London, we made an intermediate stop at Kanu, Nigeria, an interior rural area about 620 miles from Lagos. At last, we arrived in Accra. I said a prayer of thanksgiving for our safe arrival and entreated the Almighty to be with us as we embarked on this most important journey. I had no idea of what to expect. I had written to both the *Mirror* and *Graphic* newspapers and to the Amaquandoh family to alert them to our arrival, but we did not know if anyone would be at the airport to greet us. The Accra airport was a madhouse. With at least two hundred people on our flight and a KLM flight arriving a few minutes behind us, between immigration, customs, and baggage inspections, the scene was utter chaos. People were shouting everywhere in many different languages. We were immediately accosted by strangers asking if we needed a taxi or seeking to carry our luggage to a personal driver who could give us a "good rate." Although chaos to Carmen and me, it was apparent that this seeming craziness was how they routinely operated.

However, an unexpected angel waited to greet us: Mr. Apoko Acheoampong of airport security. Alerted by the newspapers that we were arriving, he took our passports and health cards and shepherded us through the chaos. There was no automation, so every job was done manually. And with piles of almost-identical suitcases stacked one upon the other, retrieving one's own for customs inspection was quite an undertaking, especially if your luggage was not near the top of the pile.

From this point until we climbed back on board for our return flight home, many of our experiences mirrored the encounters of other Western travelers in poor countries. We were greeted with hospitality as beloved family members and cheated as naïve, rich Americans who would fall for any scam or story. We rode in rickety buses and cars and vans that regularly broke down and were repaired, with equal regularity, by the amazing ingenuity of Ghanaians who worked without the proper tools or spare parts. We passed two funerals and were struck by the traditional mourning dress of beautiful, rich adinkra fabric in bright red. There were few telephones, which didn't matter much as we quickly learned that setting a time for an appointment or meeting had little meaning. We were waylaid in the outdoor markets by vendors shouting, "Look, brother! Look, sister!" and, "Cousin, have I a deal for you!" We got lost in the dark in neighborhoods where houses had no numbers and working street lights were rare. Even before we left the airport, the baggage inspector helped herself to a Quanders United T-shirt, several Amkwandoh-Quander pencils that I had custom ordered, and a selection of children's garments Carmen had purchased as barter items and gifts. We considered this action not only as low-level theft but also a bribe to let us go through without a monetary assessment. We were wrong. She directed me to leave a one-hundred-dollar "security deposit" for my Sony camcorder to ensure I was bringing it into Ghana for personal use, not planning to sell it for a sizable profit. But by the time I walked the short distance to post the deposit, the office staff demanded two hundred dollars. Hours later, at the Maple Leaf Hotel, with my printed reservation in hand, no one knew of our anticipated arrival. In addition to no reservations, we were confronted with total darkness due to a wiring short circuit, which source of difficulty had not been located or repaired. And so it went throughout our trip.

At the airport, we were met by the news editor, the feature editor, and a photographer from the *Mirror* who had come to collect us in their Land Rover. To our pleasant surprise, there were also six or seven Amaquandoh family members waiting to greet us, headed by John Alex and Isaac Amaquandoh. They had driven almost seventy miles from Cape Coast to welcome us to my ancestral homeland. Alex, who was out of work at the time, had been directed by the elders to squire Carmen and me for the duration of our trip.

Our next few days in Accra were concentrated on shopping in the Cultural Center and the Thirty-First Women's Movement Market and making calls to deliver messages and letters from Ghanaians who resided in Washington, DC. We arranged for Alex to pick us up to go shopping at 9:00 a.m. one morning, and typically, he strolled in at 12:15 p.m., which was consistent with "Africa time." We purchased several carved wooden masks and assorted Ghanaian cultural items at the Cultural Center. We needed someone to run interference for us because the prices skyrocketed the minute they saw us. Despite Alex's best efforts, we still paid significantly more for most items than would a local Ghanaian. The highlight of our Accra shopping was the downtown Thirty-First Women's Movement Market. We marveled at the women's skill in balancing large white porcelain-coated basins on their heads. Even little girls carried large flat trays in this manner. Everything anyone Ghanaian wanted in foodstuffs was there, all sorts of meats, live fowls hanging upside down by their feet, vegetables, dry goods, crabs, and even clothing and cooking utensils. It was a place of color, sights, sounds, smells, and attitudes all rolled into a blur of human activity.

The day finally arrived to travel to Cape Coast to meet the greater part of the Amaquandoh family. Dan McGaffee, U.S. Information Officer and my Omega Psi Phi fraternity brother, offered his personal car and driver to transport us to Cape Coast. John, the driver, arrived promptly—not on Africa time—at 9:00 a.m. John was a Fanti man from the village of Episidasi, which is immediately adjacent to Kankaboom, both of which are Amaquandoh ancestral villages in the Saltpond area. Along the way to Cape Coast, we encountered several military checkpoints with armed guards and gates closed across the road. But with "C.D." (*Corps Diplomatique*) license plates, we were waived through without stopping.

As we drew closer, my stomach became nervous with anticipation, wondering what lay ahead. Around noon, we arrived at the home of Agnes Amaquandoh Sagoe-Pyne, the sister of Alex, our guide. Agnes and her husband, Kobina, had moved into their beautiful, new five-bedroom home only a few months before our arrival. Agnes, a nurse in the local hospital, was happy and excited that we had come. Although we had intended to stay in a hotel—the American way of doing things—Agnes insisted that all such hotel talk should cease, as we were to be her guests.

In the afternoon, Carmen and I were taken to the Cape Coast home of Ebenezer Amaquandoh, Joseph Kojo and Ernest Kweku Amaquandoh's father, who died in 1988 or 1989 at age eighty-six years. He was the patriarch of the Amaquandoh family in the town and very much wanted to hold on to life until we got to Ghana. We were told that in 1983, after the article "American Family in Search of Its Roots" appeared in the *Mirror* and the *Graphic*, Ebenezer declared the house as the "Amaquandoh Memorial House." There we met Philip Amaquandoh, another of Ebenezer's sons, as well as a brigade of grandchildren, nieces, nephews, and cousins. At least twenty-five Amaquandohs were present. We passed out pencils and the first of two thousand balloons we had brought from home, both imprinted with "Triumphant Amkwandoh-Quander Reunion."

We were told one of the men present, Oliver Amaquandoh, was a brother of Alex, but Alex did not seem to know him. A discussion ensued about how that was possible, during the course of which I heard that Ebenezer, Alex and Oliver's grandfather, had so many children that the grandchildren might not know each other. It became clear that *brother* was used in an extended family sense, leaving it likely that Alex and Oliver were cousins, not brothers, in my American frame of reference. It was also readily apparent and disappointing to me that the people here did not have the same thirst we African Americans do for our family histories and ancestral roots. Although they talked about the ancestors, there seemed to be no real interest in getting to know their fellow descendants and who they were and how they were related. Most of the family who traveled with us to the ancestral village of Kankaboom the next day admitted they had never been there before to see where their ancestors came from. As I was told more than once, "We've been here hundreds of years, and we all are related somehow, so we really don't worry or wonder about it." Still they proudly proclaimed they were all from one ancestral Amkwandoh root, despite their general ignorance about their ancestors, and claimed me and all the American Quanders as part of the family.

Word quickly spread that the American Quanders had arrived, and later that day, after dinner at Agnes and Kobina's house, at least twenty more Amaquandohs arrived to greet me and Carmen. Meeting each of them was a very emotional time for me. There was not a dry eye in the house, as everyone was deeply touched. I told them the story Joseph Kojo and Ernest Kweku Amaquandoh told me in my living room in February 1984 about Egya Edoum Amkwandoh's being snatched on the road between Kankaboom and Episidasi, which many of them had never heard. I was surprised that the current generation did not know the story sent to me by the elders of Kankaboom. Although they were all pleased to meet the American visitors, their lack of familiarity with a fundamental family story reflected their lack of interest in their history. Fortunately, not everyone shared their lack of interest. Samuel Botwe, who served as our translator in Cape Coast and whose mother was an Amaquandoh, not only verified the story I had just told, but also he requested that we form a circle and pour libation. Samuel wanted us all to give thanks for this joinder of the Amaquandoh and Quander ancestors and their progeny in this place, now coming full circle to reunite the spirits of the separated ones. After prayer and several family members saying a word or two of thanks and appreciation, we made plans to visit the ancestral area the next day. I came to appreciate that prayer was a part of the Amaquandoh and Ghanaian family life. The Amaquandohs were almost all Christian, mostly Methodists.

Having had a long and arduous day traveling from Accra, visiting the Amaquandoh Memorial House, and meeting so many new family members, I relished a chance to get some shut-eye. But beginning at 3:30 a.m. and at seven- to ten-minute intervals thereafter, a rooster crowed. He continued this racket until 6:00 a.m. when I got up from the bed in disgust.

Already the house was bustling. Several family members arriving for the group departure had brought items for dinner, which would be prepared upon our return. A live chicken adorned a basket filled with plantains, yams, cassava, rice, beans, okra, pineapples, and ingredients for peanut soup. Seeing the chicken, for a brief moment, I visualized the crowing rooster in its place in the cooking pot. Someone also brought a young goat. The group decided to go to the ancestral village of Kankaboom. The evening before, there was lively discussion about which village to visit, and I had realized that the focus was the Saltpond area rather than a single village. When I suggested visiting more than one village, I was informed that one was all we could manage in a day because of the time we needed to complete a proper visit. It seemed the way we did things back home, the pop call, the short visit, was not possible in Africa where time, schedules, and agendas were significantly less important.

Rohulamin Quander, front row center, with
Amaquandoh cousins, Cape Coast, Ghana, 1991

Carmen decided the morning commotion was the right time to distribute the thirty Quanders United T-shirts we brought from home. Everyone was delighted, and a minor grabbing and pulling session ensued. Fortunately, everyone got one. We kept a few in case we met someone later we really wanted to give a T-shirt to.

The emotion and excitement increased as we prepared to set off. This visit to the ancestral village of Egya Edoum Amkwandoh, I believed, would be the high point of the trip, even though I could not emphatically claim that Egya of Kankaboom was our exact ancestor. I have always hedged on this point, although others, particularly journalists, have not hesitated to make that assertion. I have always named the Amkwandohs as the correct ancestral family rather than asserting that Egya founded the American Quander line. Regardless, I was setting off for where the Quanders started. Prayer was offered for a safe journey, and because of the true spiritual significance of the journey, Samuel Botwe entreated all Amaquandoh ancestors to come with us, and I entreated all the Quander ancestors to do the same.

Seventeen of us piled into the rickety van bus that had been borrowed to make the journey to Kankaboom, some twelve miles away. As we followed the main coast road back toward Saltpond, the reverse of the route we had taken yesterday from Accra, Carmen commented on the number of children working on this Sunday morning. We couldn't imagine our own children—Iliana, Rohulamin, and Fatima—working in the fields, transporting large items on their heads, and cleaning the yards and barns. Life in the United States had made us all soft.

In forty-five minutes, we turned off the main road in Saltpond and headed into the interior on a narrow, bumpy road said to be the original footpath to the main ancestral area. The Kankaboom villagers were there to greet us in full force, having learned of our imminent arrival earlier that morning from a messenger. But the suddenness of the occasion only added to their enthusiasm. Like many Ghanaian villages, this one lacked not only telephones but running water and electricity. All water was retrieved from a nearby stream, which required daily trips down a slope and ferrying heavy buckets up the hill. Candles and torches and the sun served for illumination.

We were escorted to the ancestral room, which was set aside for special occasions like funerals and when something of great significance occurred. After an animated welcome from the village elders and because the space was both dark and small, we were escorted to an open courtyard, where we were formally introduced to and received by the village chief, Nana Kwegyir the Eleventh. Several welcoming remarks were offered in Fanti, translated by Samuel Botwe, after which libation was poured thanking the Almighty for this assembly and entreating the ancestors for guidance and strength to carry forward our mission of continuing to unite the current Amaquandoh-Quander descendants. One of the village elders briefly disappeared and then returned holding a charcoal drawing high above his head. Through Samuel, he asked if I knew the depicted person. I most certainly did—it was my dad, James W. Quander. The drawing had been sent to Ebenezer Amaquandoh by his son, Kojo, from Washington, DC, and had found its way to Kankaboom after Ebenezer's death.

After libation, the men were invited to see the stool of authority for the village. The stool is more than three hundred years old and only brought out annually for veneration. We progressed to a stone-walled grotto at the end of which was a locked wooden gate. The gate was opened, and there, sitting on a cement ledge, were both the stool of authority and a smaller carved wooden stool. It was explained to me that this stool and the smaller fifteen-inch-tall piece were created in the 1600s during the great Fanti-Asanti wars. In those turbulent times, driven by outside political forces that pitted Fantis and Asantis against one another, there was a need for the tribal chiefs to meet with one another and with their own people. The portable stool of authority and the person sitting on it symbolized that despite the rancor and uncertainty of the times, the leadership was not totally bereft of stability and cultural standards when it came time to make needed decisions. The smaller stool was created by one of the earliest Fanti chiefs, all whom were Amkwandohs, as a seat for his most trusted advisor, who happened to be his wife. I was told this was unusual, as women of that era generally played no significant role in advising men in matters of war. But in this exceptional case, it was appropriate that she be given a specific item upon which to sit, it being symbolic to be seated when war and counsel were discussed.

Prayer was offered, and libation was again poured. I was told, more than once, that for more than three hundred years the residents of Kankaboom had entreated the spirit of Egya Edoum Amkwandoh to come and be with them, and they truly believed that his spirit was present that day in my person as a fulfillment of their expectations. Since seeing the article in the *Mirror* in 1983 about my search for ancestral roots, they knew their long-standing prayers would be answered. I thanked everyone for their intense and continued prayers and noted that the circle, which was broken more than three hundred years ago, was now rejoined. I paid tribute to Egya Edoum Amkwandoh and all Amaquandohs and Quanders everywhere and specifically named my father and Henry and Margrett Pugg Quando, among others, as my most regarded ancestors. After giving a brief history of the Quando-Quander family in the United States, I noted that we were like a tree with one strong trunk that emanated from strong and diversified roots and spread out into many branches. I wrapped up my remarks with the Quanders United motto, "We are many, but we are one!"

At this point, I heard drums, and upon exiting the grotto, I noted a small drum band playing and people dancing. Carmen and I were gathered up and joined the group. Although dancing, Carmen distributed candy, balloons, and pencils. In return, I was given a bottle of water from the Kankaboom stream as a memorial of this day and this visit. That bottle of water sits in my home today, treasured as a continuing connection to who my ancestors were, where they came from, and my continuity with the people of Kankaboom.

As we prepared to leave after a three-hour visit, I gathered my thoughts and wits about me and looked around to see where I came from. Life was simple and hard here. Yet the people seemed happy and content in knowing who they were and feeling a love for the simple life. Their existence was far, far from anything I had ever known, yet I thought that if I had grown up here and been a part of this community, I too would have been well adjusted to it. To leave the ancestral village that day was emotional, as was the entire trip. I felt deeply within myself a sense of place and a yearning to know and see more.

I could not be constantly angry about slavery, as that was long ago, and I have to deal with situations as they are today. Still it was difficult to turn over in my mind what the transported ancestors suffered, their abduction and pain and anguish. But I held fast to my thoughts of their determination and achievements against impossible odds, which made it possible for all of us to be here that day. I said my good-byes and told everyone that I sincerely hoped one day to return to them and to bring other Quander family members with me.

We piled back into the small bus and headed back to Cape Coast. The bus broke down, forcing all of us to stand on the side of the dusty road. Ghanaian ingenuity prevailed, and after some rigging and a lot of banging under the hood, some adjustment was made to the carburetor that allowed us to get back to Agnes and Kobina's lovely home. Once there, dinner preparation was undertaken. No fast food here, as everything must be prepared from scratch, the traditional Ghanaian way. While the food crew toiled in the kitchen and outside in the yard making fufu and kenkey, Alex called a meeting for the purpose of structuring an Amaquandoh Family organization. The Amaquandohs had expressed nothing but admiration for Quanders United and how much research and family history had been successfully completed to bring Carmen and me to be with them that day. But what started as a discussion broke down into arguments. They weren't necessarily hostile to each other, but I could not readily understand the comments as they were in Fanti. The discussion was intermittently translated for me, with more details provided later that evening. They disagreed over what type of organization there should be, who would lead it, what officers they should have, and how they could elect anyone to serve considering that large sectors of the extended family were not present.

The Amaquandohs also couldn't agree on whether their group's lead ancestor, Ebenezer Amaquandoh, had died in 1988 or 1989, nor on how many children and wives he had, with numbers varying from forty-eight to more than one hundred children by three main wives and several other women. The result was an often repeated realization that no one really knew who was descended from him and that they could not presume to represent them today without at least trying to learn who some of these people were. Even without understanding Fanti, listening to and watching the group was like watching a Ghanaian reenactment of Quander Family Reunion and Quanders United squabbles and disagreements, amusing and irritating at the same time.

Dinner that day was a traditional Ghanaian meal—stewed chicken, yams, plantains, cassava, kenkey, fufu, peanut soup, okra stew with pieces of fish in it, rice and beans, and fresh pineapple. The chicken we had seen arrive that morning was now on our plates, and Carmen couldn't bear to eat it. "I can't eat this chicken," she said to me quietly. "I knew this chicken. If I try to eat it, my stomach will turn." We quickly exchanged my bare chicken bone for her uneaten drumstick. If the others saw what we did, they did not let on.

By 5:30 p.m., we were off to the Castle of St. George at Elmina with our escort Alex and his son in a taxi. A fare argument ensued in Fanti, and we exited the taxi after a short distance without paying and took another one, leaving Alex's son at his mother-in-law's house along the way. Another argument ensued with the second cabdriver. With so many stops along the way, by the time we arrived, it was dusk, and the Elmina Castle was closing. We would have to return the following day. To us as Americans, time was money, and wasted time was lost money. Carmen and I didn't like what we saw as a wasted trip. The Ghanaians' slow pace ran contrary to much of what we treasured as calculated efficiency.

That night, I was awakened at 4:15 a.m. by the crowing roaster, which was a modest improvement over the previous night's 3:30 a.m. wakeup call. The day brought a new living food problem. That morning, as we prepared to return to the Elmina Castle, Carmen learned that the young goat that was brought to the house yesterday, a gift for her, was not a gift in the American sense but rather an offering given to her, as is the custom when someone of esteemed worth arrived. It was the intent of the offering party that the kid would be killed and eaten in a meal taken together, a traditional Ghanaian way to celebrate a special occasion. Carmen was beside herself and insisted that the kid be spared. She offered money to buy a female goat. They agreed not to kill the kid and to buy him a mate so that a whole tribe of little goats could be produced. The Amaquandohs' only concern was that there was no meat for dinner. I could not help but ask myself what insult we visited upon our hosts by insisting the kid not be killed. Eventually, the matter was dropped, but I am certain there was much discussion about it after we left the house and even after we left the country. Still less than a year after we returned home, it was reported to us that the spared goat and his new partner had produced several kids.

With the exception of the goat, the day started out like other days on our trip. Alex was on Africa time and arrived almost ninety minutes late to return us to the Elmina Castle. When we finally arrived and I saw the slave castle bathed in brilliant sunlight, I had no idea how emotional the day's events would prove to be.

Elmina Castle, Cape Coast, Ghana, where Quander
ancestors were transported to the Maryland colony

Our tour guide told us construction on the castle began in 1482 and that it was initially intended to store the food and commodities needed by Portuguese traders who were looking for a route to the Indies. Within a few years, the castle was expanded to become a slave warehouse as the Portuguese took over the growing West African slave trade. At its height, the European slave trade had forty-two slave castles, thirty-six of which were located in Ghana, and fourteen of those in the Accra area. Millions of slaves were processed through this country during the slavery era. We saw the dungeons where the slaves were held and the torture areas where they were disciplined often for no reason other than the governor's or prison guards' pleasure. Standard procedure included parading the captured women before the governor, the officers of the fortress, and visiting merchants. This group also included the priests and other clergy who officially professed celibacy and high moral character. After the women were forced to walk through the courtyard, often naked, the ones selected were directed to climb ladders that led from the courtyard to an upper level where they were given a bath before being sent to a bed-chamber to become victims of the men who chose them. The ladder was used because the women were not considered worthy enough to ascend the castle's steps and pass through its rooms. For me, the most disheartening component of this disrespect for the women's dignity was that even the clergy freely engaged in sexual misconduct.

Pregnancies were frequent. Initially, many of the impregnated slaves were freed, but as the slave trade picked up and their value was reassessed in terms of being able to get two for the price of one, many of these victimized women were shipped out on the slave ships. Some were shipped before it was known they were pregnant. Others, visibly pregnant at the time of their forced departure, delivered during the crossing.

The castle space formally designated as the church, constructed in the mid-1480s as a Roman Catholic chapel, was a lesson in true hypocrisy. Daily mass and regular confessions were offered to serve the spiritual needs of the Portuguese slave traders and operators of the slave castle while their darker-skinned brothers and sisters cried out for justice and mercy. As a Roman Catholic from one of Maryland's oldest Black Catholic families, seeing the inhumanity visited upon my Black brothers and sisters was a severe test of my faith in the church. I understood more clearly that day why so many of my contemporaries had left the church and why so many others rightfully attacked it for its long history of racism and for times when there was an obligation to speak up to prevent injustices yet little to nothing was either said or done.

Portuguese missionaries established the earliest Christian missions in Elmina, preaching the gospel and introducing the first prolonged contact with Christianity in the area. It seems ironic that the area witnessed the enslavement of Africans on the one hand, but baptism, the consecration to one God, and the promise of heaven on the other. Further—despite Kojo Amaquandoh's earlier reluctance to admit African involvement—all too often, the new Black Christian converts cooperated with the slave catchers, and either sold or arranged for the sale of their fellow Africans into permanent bondage. The concepts of nationality, racial identity, and cultural unity were unknown to the warring tribes that were selling each other's tribal members during this prolonged period of wars, of which the Ashanti-Fanti conflicts were most remembered. The lines of any fraternal affinity became blurred, which allowed Europeans to drive a wedge between the tribes, which greatly aided in the success of the slave trade.

The tour that day included seeing barred cages with stone walls and floors and what the tour guide referred to as "condemnation cells," where the slave traders generally warehoused about four hundred or more people, despite there only being room to hold fifty persons per cell. The gross overcrowding, coupled with no sanitation or ventilation, led to many deaths often from malaria. We were also shown the auction room where the bidding took place and from which the slaves were led to the ships after they had been sold. But for me, the most emotional point of the entire tour was seeing the narrow door through which each slave exited, one at a time, and descended to the waiting ships to be transported away from their homeland forever. This Door of No Return was very narrow and low, essentially a slit cut into the stone wall, so that only one person could pass through at a time, and he or she would have to bend and turn in order to pass through. Our guide explained that the limited movement the door required would render the victims vulnerable at that precise moment and prevent any mutiny at their last moment on African soil.

In 1977, when I made my first trip to Africa, I visited Goree Island in Senegal and took the slave castle tour there. Shown their Door of No Return, I appreciated its symbolism, but I did not feel a particular emotional connection to the structure or the narrow passage. On this trip, aware of the Quander family's strong Ghanaian connection, I had a completely different experience. At that moment, standing there in the Elmina Castle, I was overcome emotionally. I felt the need to have some release, and uncharacteristically, without pausing to reflect, I began to tell the guide and everyone on our tour who I was and that I was in Ghana to reconnect with my Amkwandoh ancestors and the current generations of Amaquandohs. Explaining that my ancestor, Egya Edoum Amkwandoh, had probably passed through this very door in the 1600s, never to see his homeland again, I asserted that he was not separated from Mother Africa in mind and spirit only in flesh.

I halted and then verbally paid tribute to Egya Edoum and all other Amkwandohs and all other Africans who were enslaved and lost and whose names were known only to the Almighty. Before I knew it, tears were rolling down my cheeks, and I was unable to carry on. Not being an emotional person, I found this experience exhilarating and freeing as if I had been released from a burden that I had been bearing for a long time without knowing it. My Amaquandoh cousins—Alex, Grace, Edith, and Philip—did not become nearly as emotional as I did, but they too appreciated that this was a return to the site where the blood connection between them and their American relatives was separated into two distinct lines, one in Africa, one enslaved and taken away to America. I noticed tears in the eyes of some of the other visitors. Several Africans on the tour related to what I felt and understood what I was saying. One, a Ghanaian man, put his arm around me and said, "We are all brothers and share your sorrow and grief, and now your joy as you have come back as a token to rejoin the broken circle. Welcome home! Welcome home to Mother Africa. Everything will be all right."[2] Even the normally stoic Japanese tourists comprehended that something truly spiritual was occurring. Their interpreter seemed to have translated at least part of what I said, as they offered me words of comfort, even if they did not themselves feel my emotional or ethnic connection.

As we exited the darkened dungeon into the sunlight of the courtyard, a few tourists were still holding their handkerchiefs, drying their eyes due to the emotional experience they had each shared with me moments before. Several Africans asked to have their picture taken with me. Some related that they wanted to be able to tell their family and friends that they were with an African American at the Elmina Castle at the moment when he emotionally connected to his Amkwandoh ancestors. I learned from my newly met African brothers and sisters that the room we had just left in the dungeon was commonly known as the Room of No Return, although it has no official name.

We toured other parts of the castle, including the tanning house, which helped to make the castle self-sufficient; the kitchens and the granary where foods were stored; the inner and outer moats, which guarded against escape by the slaves and made an assault on the castle extremely unlikely; the upper walkways and watch towers, various meeting rooms, and even the governor's bed chamber. We saw the land compasses that were used to plot the voyages to the Americas and to tell time. But nothing affected me as much standing in the Room of No Return and seeing the cruelly designed Door of No Return. Like a well-aimed bomb, the explosive force of self-realization suddenly and radically changed who I was as a Quander. My family had known for a long time that we were old Marylanders with a distinguished history; my research had shown that the extended Quander clan could trace its roots to Henry Quando in the seventeenth century. The 1984 Tricentennial Celebration brought tantalizing corroboration of hints from the 1960s that our family had originated in Ghana. The Kankaboom elders told us that Egya Edoum Amkwandoh had been taken by the slave catchers to the

Elmina Castle, and it was from here he departed and never saw Africa again, a wandering spirit far from home, until I came back more than three hundred years later to bring the spirit of his progeny to Ghana and his spirit could rest at last.

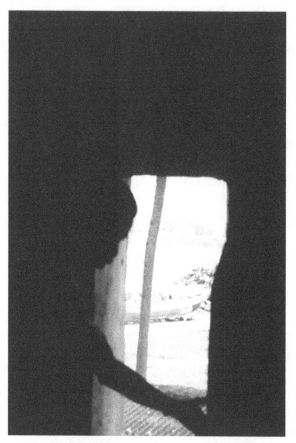

Door of No Return, Elmina Castle. It was through this door that Quander ancestors were forced to pass as they were stolen away from their Gulf of Guinea (Ghana) homeland

EPILOGUE

———— ·◆◆◆◆◆· ————

Washington, DC, 2020

As I bring this American legacy to a close, I reflect back to August 11, 1968, when I attended my first annual Quander Family Reunion. I had no real understanding of the extent and magnitude of the journey I was about to undertake. Little did I then realize that the expression "to be a Quander" would unfold in such a way, perhaps even as an obsession, and would guide the rest of my life to places and sources of knowledge that were then unknown to me. I came to realize that those West African students at Howard University who invariably called me "Mr. Quando" knew something for which I had no appreciation at the time, that there was ancestral historical treasure hidden in plain sight in being "Mr. Quando."

My journey did not occur overnight nor was it easy. Rather, it was a journey of love, much labor, and even some dead ends and disappointments. Locating verifying documents to put some meat on the skeletal remains of early and too often forgotten history was a challenge of the first order. Between the Smithsonian's Museum of American Life's Family Life Center, cousin Sandra Rattley, and me, at least one hundred interviews were conducted. Sometimes, to verify or clarify what some other family member had said, people were reinterviewed. As the decades passed and several strong threads of Quander family history emerged, I became increasingly clear as to who we really were and still are.

This clarity was achieved not so much through historical high-lights, such as noting that some ancestors were enslaved to President George Washington, and are most likely sanguinely connected to him. Nor was it particularly significant that family members distin-guished themselves in military, academic, religious, or community service callings. Rather, the Quander story is one of strong family values, focus and determination, and a deep commitment to lifting others up as we ourselves climb. We are consistently the object of others' affection and appreciation, but that enviable status carries a burden and responsibility. In examining the plight of the African American family, as influenced by a history of over four hundred years (since 1619) of obstruction, adversity, and struggle, we see that many of us lost hope or are sorely disheartened by the sustained ineq-uities in attaining full access to all that the United States of America has to offer.

A beacon, a road not otherwise taken, a signpost! That is who the Quanders are.

During our visit to Ghana in July and August of 1991, Carmen and I both had a true spiritual awakening, a fuller realization of who we really are: a son and a daughter of Mother Africa, descendants of a proud and pragmatic people whose contributions to world his-tory, culture, and society are, even now, neither fully understood nor appreciated. Visiting the Quander ancestral village of Kankaboom and the nearby Elmina Castle drew my personal journey to its logical conclusion. Standing in the Room of No Return and then touching the Door of No Return reconnected me to the millions who were involuntarily pushed or pulled through the passage as they were forc-ibly removed from their families and homelands, which they never saw again. It was an emotional moment, one that brought tears to my eyes. I could hardly get words out. Even today, over thirty years later, the emotion, the thought, and the anger of what happened to my ancestors still rage in me.

Reflecting on the story about Egya Edoum Amkwandoh and how he was snatched on the road between Kankaboom and Episidasi made me both realize and appreciate that I—Rohulamin Quander—had made the once broken circle complete again. Although Egya's flesh was unceremoniously stolen, incarcerated, and auctioned off, his spirit never died. His light was never extinguished. He was involuntarily transported to the New World, probably in the 1660s, where he found himself in a hostile and unknown place. We, the Quanders, believe he was our most probable ancestor, and even if he is not, we have maintained and expanded his spirit and memory on behalf of African people everywhere. How honored I was when Fath Ruffins, historian and curator at the Smithsonian Museum of American History, asked me to serve in an advisory capacity for the Smithsonian's photographic exhibit in Cape Coast Castle to be built around the Quander family's return to the ancestral homeland![1,2] While I have not personally seen the exhibit, several visitors to the castle have told me how informative the photographic exhibit is, often adding that they wished that they could do the same with their family histories.

In 2026, the Quanders will observe the centennial of the Quander Family Reunion. It is not too early to reflect on how far we have come since then nor to anticipate where we will be in the centennial year. Our faith in the Creator and strength as individuals and as family has carried us to this point. My greatest hope is that the family will seek and maintain a successful and blessed unity well beyond the centennial observance. Effort, commitment, and focus have characterized our past successes. These same virtues remain in demand to make the future of the Quander family mirror its past. The strength is there, only needing to be called upon. Again, may the circle remain unbroken. May the ties that have bound the extended Quander family continue to be blessed. And although we are many, may we forever be one.

The book you have just read goes well beyond the history and many stories of the Quanders. It is my deep wish that your mind and heart have been opened, able to foster a greater understanding and appreciation for what it means to be an American; to what one can achieve, despite obstacles, including issues of poverty, little formal education, and racial adversities imposed by the larger society. The Quanders did not let those obstacles stop them. Moving forward, they found a way out of a seeming no way. This is what the USA is all about: a nation comprising those who thought they could and did. I hope you have been inspired by this record of accomplishment.

We are at a crossroad, where potential authoritarian dangers and uncertainty challenge our democracy. It is up to each of us, acting both singularly and collectively, to make certain that the values we profess to share as Americans are more than words alone. I trust that in some way, *The Quander Story* contributes to your knowledge base, inspiring and ensuring the vitality of the words, "All men [and women too] are created equal."

APPENDIX

———————— ✦✦✦✦✦ ————————

Quander Achievement
and Actions of Note

Faith Communities

American history and the history of establishing faith communities in our country go hand in hand. My focus is not to recount church history but to introduce members of the Quander family who played important roles in creating and preserving these faith communities. In a number of cases, the creation of Black churches was intentionally stunted or delayed by the negative tenets of racism. Several religious leaders did not want us to succeed, did not want us to separate ourselves from their White congregations, and did all they could to dissuade us or cast us in a negative light, hoping we would lose interest or perhaps fail from the outset in our efforts to create African American faith communities.

Religious affiliation and identity were often the result of where we lived. Most of the Maryland-originated Quanders traced their religious affiliations to the Roman Catholic Church. Although religious persecution slowly crept into Maryland, restricting non-Catholic worship, from 1634, when the *Ark* and the *Dove* landed from England, Maryland was viewed as a Catholic colony, founded by the devoutly Catholic Lord Baltimore. Across the Potomac River in Virginia, however, Protestants, mainly Baptists and Methodists, held sway. Consequently, faith communities there, typified by Alfred Street Baptist Church and Woodlawn Methodist Church, were the Quander bedrock.

Sacred Heart Church, White Marsh (Now Bowie), Maryland (Founded 1729)

Although I have always assumed Henry Quando and Margrett Pugg practiced Henry Adams's Roman Catholic faith, I have not located any document linking the Quando family's association with the Roman Catholic Church from the 1600s and 1700s. I picked up the trail when I found an April 5, 1823, marriage record at Sacred Heart Church between Edward Quando and Helena Mahony, respective slaves of Master C. Waring and Master W. Watton, and with their consent. Subsequently, two baptisms were noted among this same family record, one for Sarah Anne Quander (1828) and one for Harriett Quander (1829). This early documentation underscores the desire of enslaved families to establish and maintain their families, even if spasmodically, and to practice their Catholic faith and be involved in a faith community.[1]

St. Mary of the Assumption, Upper Marlboro, Maryland (Founded 1824)

The first record book I examined at St. Mary of the Assumption covered the period 1849–1872 and noted the March 1849 baptism of Francis Quander, born on April 30, 1848, the son of William Quander and Juliana Moore. The same record listed seven additional Quander baptisms up to 1872, and later, records showed at least twenty-three baptismal references between 1873 and 1893 (some of these were cross references to the same individual). In the same journal, I noted at least fifteen Quander references to marriages, witnessing marriages, and identification of godparents. I continued my research to 1947, noting a consistent Quander family pattern of presence and participation, including a banner cycle of seven first communions between 1926 and 1928. Looking into a separate marriage register that began in 1848, I found four Quander marriages registered between 1849 and 1852.

St. Mary's Catholic Church, Upper
Marlboro, Maryland, where Quanders have
worshiped since the mid-19th Century

Looking beyond St. Mary to its affiliated mission church, Holy Rosary (located in Rosaryville in lower Prince George's County), I noted eight baptisms, two confirmations, two first communions, one marriage, and ten repeated pew rental fees paid in the parish records for 1868 through 1894.

Historic marker placed on the 1892-constructed
St. Mary's Colored Beneficial building, Main
Street, Upper Marlboro, Maryland

As my dad explained to me when I asked why Maryland-DC
Quanders didn't hold family reunions like the QFR, the history of
Quander family involvement in St. Mary's included a strong presence
in both the St. Mary's Beneficial Society (Colored) and the Knights
of St. John Commandery #74.[2] In 1908, a chapter of the Ladies
Auxiliary #21 to the Knights of St. John was introduced, likewise
dedicated to a closer spiritual alliance with their God and dedicated
to serving those in need. At least a dozen Quander women served
in various capacities. Like their brothers in the Knights, these faithful and committed women fought continuously to have the "White
only" limitations removed from certain activities that would have
otherwise continued to restrict them to participating in designated
"colored" events. An article in the January 31, 1980, issue of the
Upper Marlboro *Enquirer-Gazette o*n the occasion of the centennial
of the Beneficial noted that the Beneficial was still functioning and
serving the community. Among the office holders listed were James
A. Quander, Rachael G. Quander, Richard Eugene Quander, and
James L. Simmons, a Quander relative.

C1875-constructed home of John H. Quander and
Henrietta Tilghman Quander, and c1880s site where
St. Mary's Beneficial Society Colored, the Knights of
St. John Commandery #74, and the Ladies Auxiliary
#21 were each founded and held their earliest meetings

St. Augustine Catholic Church, Washington, DC (Founded 1858)

St. Augustine, initially known as the Blessed Martin DePorres
Chapel and School, was founded in 1858 by free and still enslaved
African Americans spurred both by a quest for literacy and education and the desire to escape the virulent racism that characterized
St. Matthews Cathedral, their nominal "home" church. They were
tired of being relegated to the back of the church, a balcony, or the
basement. In 1876, these faithful Catholics finally erected their first
church building after praying, planning, and saving their funds since
1858. In 1864, President and Mrs. Lincoln donated to the cause.
Their cancelled check is held in the church archives. The faithful's
stalwart effort and strong desire to create a visible Catholic presence
created a lasting Catholic community, including the eventual spawn-
ing of other predominantly African American Catholic churches in

189

Washington, DC, including St. Cyprian's (1893), Holy Redeemer (1922), Epiphany (1924), and St. Benedict the Moor (1946). St. Augustine is rightfully called the Mother Church of Black Catholics in the nation's capital. When the first of the five Colored Catholic Congresses convened on January 1, 1889, the site chosen for the four-day convocation was St. Augustine. Gabriel Quander, my great-grandfather, who then hailed from St. Mary of the Assumption in Upper Marlboro, was a delegate to this event.

My research into the baptismal, marriage, confirmation, and funeral records confirmed a strong Quander presence from the late nineteenth century, plus occasional notations of a Quander presence even before then. My review of the St. Augustine archives also verified the active membership and participation of numerous Quanders in diverse parish organizations, including the Holy Name Society (men), the Sodality of the Blessed Virgin Mother (men and women), the altar guild, Ladies of Charity, and many other church-related activities and events.

My wife Carmen and I are currently active in St. Augustine.

Peter Mercer Quander Sr. (1896–1976)
Holy Redeemer Catholic Church, Washington, DC
(Founded 1922)

I have combined Peter Mercer Quander with Holy Redeemer because the church is inextricably linked to the man. The true worth of any individual is not measured in terms of money or high positions attained. Such was the case with Peter, whose activism, visibility, and dedication to the uplift of his race serve as a bright beacon. A devout adherent to the Roman Catholic faith, despite local churches' attitudes toward Negroes, Peter was a cofounder of the Holy Redeemer Catholic Church and later founded its Holy Name Society, where he served as president for over thirty years. Additionally, he was a member and later the president of the Knights of St. John Commandery #218 (St. Cyprian's Roman Catholic Church) and also colonel and presiding officer of the Grand Commandery, which oversaw several of the colored commanderies throughout the Washington, DC, metro area. Active from the 1920s with the Federated Colored Catholics of the United States, on occasion, he addressed the community in a local radio program titled, "Faith of Our Fathers."

Corporal Peter Mercer Quander, Sr.,(1896-1976)
in World War I, U.S. naval uniform, 1919

After a sustained period of unrest and with the continuing insults at the hands of their fellow White parishioners from the St. Aloysius Catholic Church, several members of the colored Catholic faithful elected to call a meeting of their peers after a Sunday evening mass in November 1919. The seven designated leaders, all men, decried their continued racial mistreatment at the hands of their fellow White parishioners, which included segregated seating in the back of the church; not being able to participate in or become members of the church's auxiliary groups and activities, including the annual May procession, which honored the Blessed Mother; not being allowed to have a parallel may procession of their own; no consistent meeting room space for the colored Catholics; a pattern of verbal insults; and the greatest of all insults, having to wait to receive the Blessed Sacrament until all the Whites had been provided for. This open discrimination was the basis for Black Catholics referring to themselves as "a church in chains."

Peter Mercer Quander, who had just returned from Europe where he served our nation in the U.S. Navy (colored) during World War I, was one of the seven leaders. He maintained a minute book that recorded the emergence of this church from this initial assemblage then designated only as "the new colored Catholic Church" to "Holy Redeemer" in 1922. In his recorded minutes, Peter referred to himself as the "secretary for the new colored Catholic Church."

Of all the church records that I consulted in writing this text, Peter's were the most complete in terms of explaining how a church community went from concept to reality. The minute book shows a secular approach to realizing a goal that lets us understand the human side of founding a church. It was not just a record of masses and novenas. It was church outings, Easter dances, picnics, boat rides, and menu planning as well as controversies about "secret meetings," how funds were being handled and accounted for, and parishioners asking for their money back due to having been "misled" about whether certain approaches to problem solving were the best path to take. Some of the planned activities did not meet with financial success, requiring planners to dig into their own pockets to cover expenses. Most importantly, Peter's minute book reflects the ongoing effort and unceasing determination to make a new church building become a reality. The edifice was deemed to be complete, with blessing and cornerstone placement, on March 20, 1922.

Among those mentioned in Peter's minutes as integral contributors to building the new Black Catholic Church were several Quander family members, including Mary Blackstone Quander, Peter's wife; Charles E. and Adeline Quander Colbert, Peter's brother-in-law and sister; John Henry Quander, Peter's brother; and Veronica Quander Jennifer, Peter's sister.

In a videotaped interview, Marie Lee Hughes (b. 1915), a member from the 1922 inception of Holy Redeemer, recalled the White opposition to the new Black church, which included filing a written protest and complaint with James Cardinal Gibbons, archbishop of Baltimore, and the many negative racial epithets that seemed to roll so easily off the White people's tongues toward us as a race. She also stated, "Of all the initial church leaders, Peter and his wife, Mary Quander, dedicated their whole lives to the building of our church." In a separate interview, Louise Roberts (b. 1908), also an initial member, commented that undoubtedly Peter and Mary Quander were among the most outstanding and involved leaders of the faith community.

St. Cyprian's Roman Catholic Church, Washington, DC
(Founded 1893)

With the end of the Civil War in April 1865, many African Americans migrated to Washington, DC, in search of opportunities for jobs, housing, education, formal marriages, and creating structured families. Many of these newcomers were Black Catholics who came to St. Peter's Catholic Church, seeking to practice their religion as they had always done in Maryland. They were disappointed in this hope. They were denied full access and participation to parish activities. They had to sit in the back of the church, use a mandated "colored entrance door," were excluded from coming to the main sanctuary floor and altar, and—as at St. Aloysius—had to wait until all the Whites received communion before they were given the Holy Eucharist. In some instances, they were required to get married or be baptized at a location other than the main altar. Some of my forebears endured this shabby treatment. A cross section of St. Peter's parish records showed six Quander baptismal records between 1865 and 1882.

In 1892, after a series of letters exchanged between James Cardinal Gibbons, archbishop of Baltimore, which included the diocese of Washington, DC, and James Matthews and J. M. O'Brien, two sympathetic White priests stationed at St. Peter's, permission was granted to form a separate parish for the colored faithful.

The name selected for the new church, St. Benedict the Moor, was later changed to St. Cyprian. Both were African saints. Alexander

Young, a stone mason, was integrally involved in the physical construction of the church. His wife, Elizabeth Quander Young, was one of a cadre of church women who worked tirelessly during the construction to supply the men with good meals, thus reducing the amount of time the construction crew was off site. In many cases, the men had day jobs as well and worked on the church building after hours, generally with the aid of light provided by torches. Beyond Alexander and Elizabeth, the presence of the Quander family was well established at St. Cyprian's. Baptismal (1892–1922) and marriage (1892–1945) records showed sixteen Quander-related baptisms, including that of James William Quander, my father. As well, I found nine marital records, one of which was for my grandparents, John Edward and Maude Beatrice Pearson Quander, married on August 23, 1905.

St. Benedict the Moor Roman Catholic Church, Washington, DC (Founded 1946)

Much as the Civil War changed Washington, DC, from a sleepy southern town into a busy, crowded city, with the coming of World War II, the city quickly converted to a national capital of a country at war. One consequence of this change was an influx of African Americans, particularly from nearby Prince George's, Charles, and St. Mary's Counties, where Catholicism had a long-established presence. The new arrivals looked for Catholic churches where they would feel both welcome and "at home." They found neither. At the White-majority churches, more often than not, they had to sit in segregated seating, could not enjoy the sacrament of the Holy Eucharist until the Whites had first been served, and were unable to belong to the parish organizations that were the underlying basis for socialization and developing a sense of being fully invested church members. As the recently arrived colored faithful often said, "The unwelcome mat was well laid out."

In 1944, at Holy Name, my father James W. Quander encountered such an experience when he complained to the White priest during confession that he was tired of being a second-class parishioner. He asked the priest why, in this supposedly equal world, was the Catholic Church so racist to the core? The priest took umbrage to my dad's query and tried to brush it off, adding that God made man and put him in certain places and perhaps if they had stayed in their places as designated, there would be no need to have this conversation.

Incensed, James told the priest in a voice loud enough for everyone waiting to go to confession to hear every word, "How dare you! If the White man had kept his pants zipped up instead of raping our women and dragging us in the holds of slave ships to this racist country, none of this problem would have happened!" And with that, he stormed out. Later, he told me that he was certain that the colored parishioners who were waiting near him before entering the confessional booth knew quite well what had caused his angry outburst.

James wasn't the only person thoroughly tired of the status quo. A crescendo was building among the colored faithful. They wanted their own Catholic Church in their own neighborhood. Charles Johnson Quander and several other exasperated Quander family members joined a cadre of other leaders who pursued the realization of a new African American church. This core group—which included Charles's wife, Alyce; John Edward Quander and his wife, Helen Orena Stuart Quander; and John and Helen's daughter, Evelyn Quander Rattley—would be identified as the founders of St. Benedict the Moor. After detailed correspondence between Archbishop Curley of the Archdiocese of Baltimore and the founders, the archbishop agreed that there should be a new colored Catholic parish.

On April 17, 1946, Passion Sunday, the first mass was celebrated at St. Benedict the Moor. My dad told me I attended, although I cannot recall being there. The new church was nurtured by the ongoing participation of Charles and Alyce, John and Helen, and other Quanders. I believe it can be accurately said that the apex of the Quander family as members of the Roman Catholic faith community was reached in their participation in establishing and maintaining St. Benedict the Moor.

*Alfred Street Baptist Church, Alexandria, Virginia
(Founded 1803)*

Alfred Street Baptist Church, Old Town
Alexandria, Fairfax County, Virginia, where
Quander legacy traces to c1813

The Quander family has been an integral part of the Alfred
Street Baptist Church community from the outset, beginning with
President George Washington's former enslaved, Nancy Carter
Quander, whose offspring were counted among the earliest membership. Mariah Quander joined the faith community in the early
1800s, and other early records from 1807 and 1813 show a Quander
connection. Quander participation increased in the early 1900s
when many Quander ancestors were baptized into and joined the
church. Among them were Mariah's son, Charles Henry Quander (c.
1843–1919), his wife, Amanda Rebecca Bell Quander (1848–1918),
and their six children. One of their sons, Robert H. Quander (1879–
1942), was an ordained deacon at Alfred Street for many years. He
and his wife, Sadie Chinn Quander (1889–1975), had three chil-

dren: Emmett (1919–83) who served as a trustee; Grayce (1922–68) who was chair of the finance committee for many years; and Roberta H. (1924–2020) who assumed that same position upon Grayce's death and served for more the twenty-five years.

Another of Charles Henry and Amanda's sons, James Henry Quander (1882–1971), joined Alfred Street around 1900 and is remembered for arriving by horse-drawn wagon to attend evening church services after the daily farm chores were completed. The many contributions of James Henry's daughter, Gladys Quander Tancil, to the Quander family are discussed above. In addition, Gladys was involved in several Alfred Street ministries, including the Sunday school program and historical research to document how Alfred Street came to be. Her brother, Welton (1925–2011), was a faithful member of the Alfred Street community for seventy-five years, serving on the Deacon Board for twenty-five years and the Board of Trustees for thirty-one years.

Many other Quanders and Quander relatives have sustained Alfred Street over the years as active members of the congregation by participating in the numerous committees running a large church requires; contributing their skills to the church's ministries and fund drives; and serving as ushers, choir members, musicians, and Sunday school and vacation Bible school teachers. Alfred Street was also part of the early QFR. The QFR founders recognized from the outset that a religious component should be a necessary part of each annual reunion. Andrew Warren Adkins, who served as pastor from 1920 until 1963, frequently attended the early reunions.

Mount Calvary Baptist Church, Spring Bank, Virginia (Founded 1953)

Mount Calvary Baptist Church started small and grew strong.[3] The temporary meeting places for the congregation included a mobile trailer, the garage, and a tent until land was purchased in 1954, and two church buildings were completed within twenty-three months. From its outset in 1953, several Quander family members were instrumental in establishing Mount Calvary Baptist Church's history and legacy. Deacon George Williams, husband of Pearl Quander Williams, served as the construction chair for both the main sanctuary and the church annex building, and Ezell Hines, husband of Alcinda Quander Hines, provided plumbing services for both construction projects. The construction team of the front addition to the sanctuary included George and Pearl's sons, Trustee Joseph Williams and Lewis Williams. Charles Henry Quander Sr. and Charles Jr. both contributed their carpentry skills during the construction projects, and Harrison Quander contributed his carpentry and masonry talents to building the annex.

Not resting once the physical structures were in place, Quander family members continued as progenitors of Mount Calvary by living its missions and purpose. Harrison Quander served as the church clerk for a number of years, and in 1955, he was the first member to join the new church and was baptized. He became a trustee and later served as the financial secretary of the church. His talent and efforts resulted in the church's rapid repayment of the construction loan, which led to the burning of the first annex mortgage. Harrison's sisters, Alcinda Quander Hines and Pearl Quander Williams, served Mount Calvary in multiple roles. Both sisters served on the Deaconess Board, Senior Usher Board, Historian, and Women's Club and participated separately in the senior choir and volunteer chorus and as Sunday school teachers and in the Missionary Society. Alberta Hines Webb, Alcinda's daughter, served as chairperson of the Anniversary Committee, Church Treasurer, and the Sunshine Fellowship Ministry, an outreach community ministry. Robin Quander Whitmire currently serves as ministry chairperson for the Administrative Staff Ministry and Finance Committee. She previously served as an officer of the Women's Ministry.

The Mount Calvary Baptist Church faith community firmly believes that joy can be discovered even when the world seems unfair. The Quander family is among the many examples.

Professional and Personal Achievement

This section introduces Quanders distinguished by their accomplishments and contributions as well as Quanders who lived rich, full, productive lives while struggling with the obstacles of segregation and racial persecution. Several notable Quander family members (Gladys Quander Tancil) and ancestors (West Ford) whose lives and contributions are included above are omitted here, and a few, such as Lewis Lear Quander and my father James W. Quander, are discussed in greater detail.

John Thomas Quander, MD, (c1881-1910),
Howard University College of Medicine, Class of 1909

As a contemporary reader, you may question whether some of the accomplishments described were of notable significance, but I ask you to bear in mind that I am not referring to twenty-first-century accomplishments. Rather, some of the men and women included lived during the midnineteenth to midtwentieth centuries, a time when few African Americans were able to break through the many layers of racial discrimination and denial of access that were imposed upon them solely because of their color. Regardless of the limitations they faced, they showed what can be achieved with enduring and persistent determination, thus creating a legacy that all African Americans, not only Quanders, have inherited.

John S. Quander (1859–1924)

John S. Quander was born into enslavement in Upper Marlboro, Maryland, a son of John Henry and Henrietta Tilghman Quander. His sustained record of achievement over time was striking for the sense of purpose, focus, and dedication it illustrates. The bulk of his working life was with the U.S. Bureau of Engraving and Printing in Washington, DC, probably in a "colored job," a work category that included printer, janitorial, or clerk messenger. Like virtually all the Maryland Quanders, John S. Quander was raised in the Roman Catholic Church. He was an active member of St. Augustine and later St. Cyprian's. In later years, quite likely out of negative racially charged frustration, he allegedly left the Catholic Church but still maintained his strong Christian values. His was a life of significant accomplishment for a man who knew slavery as a child and rampant racism throughout his life.

In the parlance of the nineteenth century, John S. Quander was widely known as a "race man," one of that generation of Negroes who devoted their lives to uplifting the plight of all of us. A 1917 article in the *Washington Bee*, a local colored newspaper, described him as "a valuable Acquisition to Society—A Progressive, Liberal and a devoted Churchman and a thoughtful Race Man." The *Bee* listed nine organizations in which Quander was active, including the Washington, DC, chapter of the NAACP (executive committee) and Crispus Attucks (board of trustees). A later *Bee* article in 1920 noted that John S. Quander had completed his term as chairman of the Relief Committee of the Home Beneficial Association, one of the many organizations that emerged to help others less fortunate after the end of slavery. "Mr. Quander is a member of many organizations," the editor wrote. "He never surrenders when in a fight or in the trenches."

The pattern of contributions to civil and religious organizations that emerge from John S. Quander's life depict a man who rose above the adversities of enslavement by lifting himself up, taking many others with him in the process. The phrase, "Lift as you climb!" was nowhere more appropriate and applicable than to the life of this determined man.

John Pierson Quander, Sr., and Hannah Bruce Ford's Descendants

Nellie M. Quander was a well-recognized suffragist and community activist. She was also the first supreme basileus of the Alpha Kappa Alpha Sorority, Inc. (1911–1919). Her biography was published by Rohulamin Quander in *Nellie Quander, Alpha Kappa Alpha Pearl* in 2008.

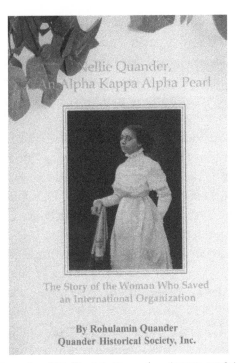

Portrait of Nellie M. Quander, (1880-1961),
First Supreme Basileus, Alpha Kappa Alpha Sorority and
leading suffragist in 1913 national Suffragist March

The next three entries are siblings, the children of John Pierson Quander Sr. (1845–1925), and Hannah Bruce Ford Quander (1850–1941). John Sr.'s life is discussed below under "Military Service and Leadership."

John Pierson Quander Jr. (1875–1957)

John Pierson Quander Jr., born in Fairfax County, Virginia, graduated from the M Street High School (now Dunbar High School) in 1893 where he served as a private in the first formally organized company of Negro cadets in the District of Columbia. Later, he worked as a newspaper correspondent for the *Brooklyn Eagle*, an office manager for the colored American newspapers, and a typing and shorthand teacher in the Washington, DC, public school system.

During the Spanish-American War, John Jr. served the U.S. government in a civilian capacity and was assigned to the Philippines in about 1900. He remained with the Philippine Constabulary for twelve years as chief accountant and was widely recognized for establishing a complete accounting system for the Philippine government. Upon his return to the United States, John worked at several financial institutions, including the Tidewater National Bank of Virginia and the Northeastern Life Insurance Company. He was also the first and only Negro bookkeeper and assistant cashier at Dunbar National Bank in Harlem, New York (1929–1932). This position was taken from him when new management did not wish to have Negroes working in such a responsible capacity.

After his forced separation from Dunbar, John founded the accounting firm of Quander and Rowlins. He is credited with being one of the first African American certified public accountants in the state of New York. Like many Quanders of his era, he was actively involved in the Masonic Lodge and was a Past Master of Eureka Lodge No. 5 of the Free and Accepted Masons of Washington, DC.

Susie Russell Quander (1881–1973)

Susie Russell Quander, born in Washington, DC, taught for forty-two years (1902–44) in the city's public school system at the elementary and junior high school levels. Believing strongly in self-improvement, she enrolled at Howard University and earned her AB degree (1926) with an academic focus on African history and civilization. A longtime member of the Association for Negro Life and History (now the Association for the Study of Afro-American Life and History), the organization that created Black History Month, she served as secretary to Dr. Carter G. Woodson for the DC branch of the organization for twelve years (1926–1938). Susie Quander was also an active member of the Zeta Phi Beta Sorority, the Order of the Eastern Star, and the M Street School Alumni Association. Her service in the Eastern Star was of particular note, as she held many elective and appointed positions from the outset of her membership (c. 1911) until her death in 1973. She was also active in the historic abolitionist-based Asbury United Methodist Church in Washington, DC, for many years.

On the occasion of her 1944 retirement, the Garnet Patterson Junior High School principal wrote, "Her chief virtues are refinement, thoroughness, neatness of both person and work, industry, dependability, and kindness. In faculty discussions and associations, she is firm with tact. In administering to human needs, she is outstandingly generous without vain glory. She is loyal without superficiality. She has preserved a wholesome sense of humor. She is tolerant without sacrificing her own high standards."

Charles Calvin Quander (1886–1957)

Charles Calvin Quander began living an interesting life early. When he was perhaps six or seven, he struck up a conversation with a passerby on the street. The man was surprised at the young child's seeming wisdom and focus. When Charles's mother came out onto the front porch, she immediately invited the man in. The offer was graciously accepted. Who was this eloquent, well-dressed man? None other than Frederick Douglass, the Great Emancipator, orator, and former enslaved. That afternoon, Douglass was just leaving Howard University after a Board of Trustees meeting. Written communications confirm that the connection between Charles and Douglass continued, although I have been unable to uncover its extent.

At fifteen, Charles left school to swing high on a trapeze and jump from hot air balloons when he joined a carnival that toured state fairs. Years later, after telling his sons of his youthful adventures, he was forced to produce the handbill he had kept promoting "happy Quander," as they could not believe their stern father had ever led such a carefree life. Charles attended Howard University Medical College for two years (1907–1909), but he dropped out and a year later rode with Pancho Villa in 1910 during the Mexican Revolution. One of his favorite stories recounted that during one of the revolutionaries' sojourns in a saloon in Mexico, when he was unaware that he could not dance with a lady unless he asked permission first from her suitor, he faced a life-threatening experience after dancing with a beautiful lady. Another man quickly came to his rescue, demanding that he give every lady in the saloon a twirl or two. Demonstrating an interest in all the ladies present disarmed what appeared to be a particular interest in a specific senorita. Thus he lived to tell the story with some enhancement each time he related the experience.

Among his many places of employment were the steel mills in Pennsylvania and the U.S. Army Academy at West Point, where he was the only Negro at the time employed as a federal government clerk. During World War I, Charles volunteered for the 15th Infantry Regiment New York Guard, later reorganized as the 369th Infantry, which even today is known as the Harlem Hellfighters, and recognized for their distinguished military service during World War I. Charles, an expert with handguns, rifles, and machine guns, remained stateside, where he helped to organize the original 369th and held the rank of Captain of Infantry in that guard. After the war, starting in 1921, he became the second African American to serve as an attendance officer in the Manhattan Division of the New York City school system.

A difficult situation arose in the 1930s while Charles was serving as a Masonic Grand Master for New York. Racial tension across the

Hudson River in New Jersey had emboldened the Ku Klux Klan to ride through local Negro neighborhoods, frightening everyone. Because of his knowledge of weaponry, Quander was called to organize two sectors of his Masonic brothers and to school them in self-defense. The Masons organized themselves under the guise of a hunting and fishing club, obtained the necessary licenses and clothing, and carried their shotguns everywhere even to church. Riding through the community one evening, intent on intimidation, the Klan was shocked when the Masons opened fire with a fusillade. Their response to the intimidation had been carefully planned, and no one was hurt, but the KKK got the message. They never returned.[4]

Charles lived by a simple motto: "Everyone you meet, you can learn something from. So don't look down your nose at anybody. Treat everyone as an equal until they decide to be treated otherwise. Learn as much as you can about everything you run into."

John Richard Quander (1908–1970)

John Richard Quander was an early African American FBI special agent in the J. Edgar Hoover Administration. Born in Washington, DC, the fourth child of Charles H. and Annie Johnson Quander, John's early life was adversely affected by the death of his mother when John was fifteen years old. With his mother gone, he dropped out of Armstrong High School where he was a jokester and cutup, which led to many suspensions. Just before leaving school, he met and fell in love with Mary Bowie, advising her that when they were both twenty-one, they would marry. During the intervening years, working low-paying factory and domestic service jobs, he regularly renewed his marriage plans with "get ready!" love letters. Sure enough, Mary and John married in 1929 when they were both twenty-one.

John worked as a do-it-all manservant for a physician who lived in the same apartment complex as FBI Director J. Edgar Hoover, who noticed John's intelligence, versatility, and professionalism and especially his capacity to fix automobiles. Associate FBI Director Charles A. Tolson, who lived in the same building, suggested John should apply for a position with the FBI, where he could maintain the fleet vehicles and serve as a chauffeur. In those days, 1942, the FBI did not hire Negroes in any other than low-level positions. Still for John to obtain a job at the FBI, especially as Hoover's personal chauffeur, was a major accomplishment. In addition to driving Hoover, Tolson, and other top-ranking officials, he frequently drove current and former political dignitaries who were in town, the most prominent of whom was former President Herbert Hoover. Finally, after chauffeuring for eighteen years, John was promoted to special agent and worked in the fingerprinting department. John worked for the FBI for twenty-eight years.

At the time of his death, John and Mary were members of Our Lady Queen of Peace. His service was scheduled to be held in the church's small chapel, but he received many voluminous flower arrangements, and when it was learned that Hoover, Tolson, and several fellow FBI employees would attend the mass, his service was moved to the main sanctuary.

Milton Ford Quander, MD (1912–1996)

Milton Ford "Jack" Quander was born in Washington, DC, the only child of John Pierson Jr. and Maude Barker Quander. He graduated from Howard University School of Medicine in 1943, and the following year was called to U.S. Army military service. In Europe, he was attached to the division's 317th medical battalion, Company D, where he administered to the wounded colored troops. Upon returning to the United States in 1946, Jack completed his internship at Harlem Hospital and subsequently opened a medical practice in obstetrics and gynecology. He was a fellow of the American College of Obstetrics and Gynecologists and likewise a diplomate of that professional organization.

Racism leaves scars. For Jack, the bitterness left by a refusal of service at a lunch counter never dissipated. As a young man, having returned from his tour of duty in Europe a few days before and proudly wearing his U.S. Army captain's uniform, he and a lady friend were refused luncheon service at National Airport, located just outside of Washington, DC. He was told by a waiter, "I'm sorry, but

THE QUANDERS—SINCE 1684,
AN ENDURING AFRICAN AMERICAN LEGACY

we don't serve colored people here." The diner's manager repeated the denial in a significantly more formal and dismissive tone. When I spoke to him years later, Jack said to me, "I was really bitter about that. Here I have just returned from overseas, serving my country and living in the face of potential death, and they won't serve me. What a shame. They played baseball and games here with White German and Italian prisoners of war and let them eat with their White counterparts, who were Caucasian Americans. They, the enemies, were treated better than our own citizens. I am just sick of it. Sick! Sick! Sick! And it was that attitude and circumstance that largely contributed to my decision to leave Washington, DC, and the South." And in spite of his professional accomplishments, I sincerely believe he carried that bitterness to the end of his life.

James William Quander (1918–2004)

In 1924, a month before his sixth birthday, James William Quander, my father, was diagnosed with diabetes. His parents, John E. and Maude B. Pearson Quander, were told their son was unlikely to live to be ten years old. But with attentive medical care and his own enthusiasm and determination, James became a disciplined person when it came to his health. Adopting the motto, "Diabetes is not a death sentence but rather a challenge to live!" he was an excellent example of how someone with an incurable ailment can live a full, active, and happy life.

James was a regular demonstrator against racial discrimination and disparity, picketing places such as Sanitary Grocery (Safeway today), Peoples Drug Stores (now CVS), and the Lisner Auditorium at George Washington University for their refusal to hire Negro employees. He was reported to the federal authorities as a "troublemaker," sparking an investigation as to whether his views were sympathetic to communism. At Miner Teacher's College, from which James graduated in 1940, the administration identified him as someone they should groom to pursue a professional position in the FBI. This effort was part of "the New Negro Movement." Miner staff helped James prepare his application and conducted a practice "hostile" interview. The real interview concluded with the White interviewer saying, "We do not hire Negroes for these [FBI] positions. We will refer your application to the U.S. Post Office." Fully expecting such a rebuff, James replied, "If I had wanted to work for the post office, I would have applied there." Everyone knew no FBI job would be forthcoming, but his Miner supporters lauded James's effort. The goal was to underscore that Negroes were just as qualified as the typical White employees the FBI was hiring. In his ensuing thirty-three-year federal service career, James worked for the U.S. Post Office, the Government Printing Office, the Office of Price Administration, the U.S. Census Bureau, the Department of Defense, and the U.S. Department of Labor.

In addition to picketing, James was a frequent Letter to the Editor writer to the *Washington Post*, the *Evening Star*, and the *Daily News* on issues of social justice, discrimination, and the need to awaken the public consciousness of the daily wrongs being committed against our race. Some of these papers considered his letters too controversial to print, but the Washington *Afro American* frequently published his comments.

James W. Quander, first row far right, with first
ever class of Roman Catholic Permanent Deacons
in the United States, September 11, 1971

208

A devout Roman Catholic, James was enthralled when he learned of the church's reinstitution of the permanent diaconate, which had been abolished over eight hundred years before. Historically, the permanent deacons were men dedicated to the cardinal works of mercy: feeding the hungry, visiting the sick and imprisoned, caring for widows and orphans, and burying the dead. He was ordained as a permanent deacon in 1971 after completing three years of intense study conducted by the Josephite priests, a member of the first class of sixteen to be ordained in the United States. Faithfully discharging his duties for the next thirty-three years, he assisted at mass every Sunday, and sometimes preached the weekly sermon; conducted marriages and funerals; took people to the doctor; served as marriage counselor, spiritual advisor, and mentor; and met with senior citizens groups. The highlight of his diaconate occurred in 1975 when he assisted Pope Paul VI in celebrating mass in Rome during the canonization week for St. Elizabeth Seton.

Lewis Lear Quander (1919–2003)

Lewis Lear Quander exemplifies those Quanders and African Americans who lived rich, full lives in the face of segregation and unflagging racism. We were blessed to have him in our family. Born in Pittsburgh, Lewis was a descendant of Nancy Carter Quander, Tobias Lear, and West Ford and the second child of an interracial marriage at a time when such marriages were usually frowned upon and outlawed upon penalty of prison in many states.

When his father Frank Quander, out of racially infused frustration, walked away, the young family was not able to survive as a unit. For several years, Lewis lived with family friends, and as a young teen, he moved to Virginia to live with his aunt, Emma Quander Harris. He left at fifteen years old, rebelling against the stern house rules of Emma and her husband. After years of riding "hobo trains" and playing in a washboard and jug band in New York collecting coins on street corners and in bars and restaurants, Lewis enlisted in the U.S. Army in 1941 and was assigned as a combat engineer to the 91st Engineers, a segregated outfit in the Pacific that, as Lewis put it, "specialized in building air strips and bridges and blowing up things." After the war, he reenlisted in 1947 in the newly created U.S. Air Force and was assigned to Special Services, where his job was to help put entertainment programs together for the airmen. During this time, he studied voice, entertained the troops as a traveling singer, and won the air force singing championship in 1953.

Retiring in 1956 as a staff sergeant, he relocated to Norwalk, Connecticut, where he became the city president of the NAACP and worked tirelessly on statewide committees for the organization. He was proud of being a thorn in the side of the city leaders who the NAACP believed were attempting to confine African Americans to certain selected neighborhoods. He withstood many threats and insults, leading his civilian troops to housing and community rights victories.

Lewis began writing poetry at an early age and won several national and international poetry competitions. Although much of his work was lost over time, in his later years, he collected some of his work in *Echoes from Past and Present: Poems* (1990). "To Be a Quander" appears below.

To Be a Quander

Dear Sir or Madam I can see
This letter that you wrote to me
Expressed a strange desire—to be a Quander.
Tell me why in heaven's name
Do you really have no shame?
Well, you'll have to bear the blame—to be a Quander.

Dear Sir or Madam, with much pain
I must reiterate again
That you would have to be insane—to be a Quander.
Not only crazy, stupid too

If you don't think this is true
Here's some things you'll have to do—to be a
Quander.

First you have to learn to fight
Most verbally...all night
And scream until you earn the right—to be a
Quander.
A Quander is a breed apart
Peculiar, but with lots of heart
You must know this before you start—to be a
Quander.

A Quander, whether fat or slim
Will satisfy his every whim
And you must go along with him—to be a Quander.
You must not ever sing the blues
But always pay your union dues
And know how to control your booze—to be a
Quander.

In final word, dear girl or man
If you can see a wedding band
And if you fit it in your plan—to be a Quander.
Good luck to you, and all the best
When all your days bring happiness
You know that you have passed the test—to be a
Quander.

Evelyn Orena Quander Rattley (1924–2020)

Evelyn Orena Quander Rattley's life is a living testimony to
Quander values: love of family, faithful dedication to her church,
education, and service to others. She was born in Washington, DC,
the only daughter of John Edward Sr. and Helen Orena Stewart
Quander. She earned a BA (education/psychology) from Howard

University, an MA (special education) from George Washington University, and completed postgraduate work at Miner Teachers College, Catholic University, and the Education for Parish Service program at Trinity University. Evelyn retired in 1977, after thirty years of service in the DC public schools as an elementary classroom teacher, education assessor, instructor of children with learning disabilities, and resource teacher/supervisor of special education. Upon retirement, she started anew and became an advocate for persons with disabilities/special needs for the Archdiocese of Washington. Her efforts were recognized in 1989 by the Howard "Rocky" Stone Award, given on behalf of the archdiocese for her leadership, service, and advocacy for disabled persons.

Evelyn served on the scholarship committee of the DC Retired Educators Association and was a director on the board of the AARP, Chapter 2414, as well as chairman of its scholarship committee. She volunteered as a docent at the National Archives for four years, where she explained the importance of documents like the Declaration of Independence and Emancipation Declaration to school children and tourists. She also served as a docent at the opening of the John F. Kennedy Presidential Library in Boston.

A founding member of St. Benedict the Moor Catholic Church (1946), Evelyn has been active in all phases of parish life since the church's beginning. In 2005, she was awarded the Order of Merit Medal from the Archdiocese of Washington for faithful service to the church. In addition, Evelyn served as president of the Council of Catholic Women, later assuming the highest office as province director; was a delegate to the World Union of Catholic Women's Organizations conference in Guadalajara, Mexico (1991); and was a member of the team that developed the "Women's Literacy for Third World Countries" initiative, which was sent from the conference to the United Nations for enactment. The Council of Catholic Women nominated her for the "Manifesting the Kingdom" award, which honors Catholics who are "unsung heroes."

In 2002, Evelyn visited Ghana, West Africa, as a gift for her eightieth birthday. One of the most moving experiences of her life was visiting the village of Dutch Komenda, one of the ancestral homeland areas. With tears in her eyes, she said, "I feel at home. I feel rejuvenated."

Loretta Carter Hanes (1926–2016)

Loretta Carter Hanes's lifetime achievements were character-ized by a devotion to youth and education, which dated back to her teenage years when a family friend, Brother Jordan, a 102-year-old ex-enslaved man, told her, "I want you to carry others across the bridge of life." As a young adult, she realized she could best fulfill that charge by helping children learn to read. Loretta was born in Washington, DC, the daughter of Joseph Washington Carter and Hattie Louise Thompson Carter, and was thus a direct descendant of Sukey Bay and her daughters Rose Carter and Nancy Carter Quander, enslaved women at George Washington's Mount Vernon Plantation. After earning a bachelor's degree in education from Miner Teacher's College (1949), Loretta devoted her professional life to being an edu-cator, historian, researcher, community activist, and environmental public health advocate.

Loretta taught in the DC public schools after her graduation, and in the mid-1960s, she joined the DC Citizens for Better Public Education, which launched a children's literacy pilot project in 1966 that became the nationally recognized Reading Is Fundamental (RIF) program. Loretta joined the DC RIF Board of Directors in 1974 and, in 1981, was named director of DC RIF, where her work led to the reenergizing of reading motivational programs for nearly seventy thousand youngsters. Loretta served as the DC RIF president/direc-tor until her death.

In 1990, WUSA-TV 9, the local CBS-TV affiliate, honored Loretta with the One and Only Nine Award and the Jefferson Award from the American Institute for Public Service for her accomplish-ments in promoting literacy. In 1991, National RIF awarded Loretta with its highest honor, the Distinguished Volunteer Service Award, recognizing her seventeen years of work in motivating young people to read. In the mid-1990s, Barbara Bush, who chose literacy as her special cause, hosted a reception at the vice president's house, honoring Loretta and exceptional DC RIF school coordinators.

A family genealogist and student of Washington, DC, history, Loretta contributed family tree research and loaned heirloom china with a distinctive blue willow pattern, similar to the shards of china with a blue willow pattern excavated from Mount Vernon's slave quarters, to the Smithsonian National Museum of American History's 1985–2002 exhibit, *After the Revolution: Everyday Life in America, 1780–1800*. The same china was part of *Lives Bound Together: Slavery at George Washington's Mount Vernon*, a 2016–2020 exhibit at Mount Vernon.

While researching for the DC Bicentennial Commemoration (1791–1991), Loretta uncovered DC Emancipation Day historical materials, commemorating President Abraham Lincoln's signing the DC Compensated Emancipation Act into law on April 16, 1862, which ended slavery in the district and compensated slaveholders for the enslaved they once held. Subsequently, the National Archives announced it would annually display both the Emancipation Proclamation and the DC Emancipation Act. For her outstanding work on DC Emancipation history educational issues, Loretta received numerous awards, including a certificate of U.S. Congressional Special Recognition in the mid-1990s; the DC Mayor's DC Emancipation Distinguished Service Award (2004); and the DC Council DC Emancipation Day Award for Distinguished Service (2015). The DC Mayor's Loretta Carter Hanes DC Emancipation Day Awards Program was held in her honor in April 2013.

Nellie Brooks Quander (1930–2019)

Nellie Brooks Quander, the only daughter of Rev. and Mrs. Houston G. Brooks of Alexandria, Virginia, broke many racial and gender barriers during her long career as an educator. She graduated from segregated Parker Gray High School (1948) and earned her bachelor's degree from Virginia Union University (1952). Upon graduation, she was hired as an elementary school teacher in the still segregated Alexandria public school system. While Nellie continued her teaching career, she obtained a master's degree in education administration and an education specialist degree, both from George Washington University in Washington, DC.

Nellie achieved many firsts. After the schools were desegregated, Nellie was the first African American to be appointed to an administrative position at Cory Kelly Elementary School. She also served as principal at Charles Houston Elementary School and Jefferson-Houston Elementary School. She was the first African American woman in Virginia to be invited to join the Delta Kappa Gamma Education Society International. In 1970, she was elected as the first African American woman president of the twenty-five-thousand-member National Association of Elementary School Principals. The following year, 1971, she was selected to travel to China for an educational comparison tour of Chinese public school education, from preschool to the university level, with traditional public education in the United States. After China, Nellie held other positions in Fairfax County, which included service as coordinator of Elementary Education, Administrative Assistant to the Superintendent, and Administrator of Area I Schools. From 1986 to 1994, she served on the state board for community colleges.

Her many awards and recognitions include Educator of the Year for the Northern Virginia Chapter of Phi Delta Kappa; Administrator of the Year, Fairfax Association of Educational Office Personnel; and Educator of the Year, Virginia Association of Elementary School Principals. Nellie's contributions to improving public education included conducting seminars and workshops at the elementary school level, addressing educators on best practices and writing publications designed to improve the teaching skills of both new and experienced teachers. In 1993, Northern Virginia Community College conferred upon Nellie an Honorary Associate Degree in Humane Letters, a state recognition of her having achieved significant success in her personal and public life. In December 2016, she served as the grand marshal of the Campagna Center's 46th Annual Scottish Christmas Walk Parade held in Old Town Alexandria. When I asked Nellie about paying homage to Scottish ancestry, she said, "It was a wonderful opportunity to be a Black woman heading this virtually all-White parade. It shows just how far we have come. It was indeed an honor."

Joseph Pearson Quander Jr., MD (1934–)

Joseph Pearson Quander Jr., MD was born in Washington, DC, the eldest of the three children of Joseph Sr. and Algetha Warfield Quander. As an African American youth growing up in the Brookland neighborhood, his daily lot was typical—trekking across town to a "Negro school" because no schools in the immediate area would enroll colored students. He made the best use of his time, however, and—after his graduation from Dunbar High School, Yale, Harvard, and Notre Dame universities—offered Joseph substantial scholarships. He chose Yale, one of only two Negro students in the class, and—after graduation—enrolled in the Howard University College of Medicine. He completed an internship at DC General Hospital, Washington, DC, followed by a two-year surgical residency. Joseph entered the U.S. Air Force in 1964 with assignments to Georgia and Texas. After completing his military obligation as a captain, he pursued an obstetrics-gynecology (OB-GYN) residency in 1966.

In Texas, several older African American physicians urged Joseph to relocate to Austin to establish his practice with them as their ob-gyn specialist. At the time, there were very few African American doctors in Austin, a city of several hundred thousand. As he and his wife, Arthuree, were making plans to relocate, he was invited by the University of Texas Health Center in Austin to assume a staff position in his specialty with the added incentive that he would be the first African American medical doctor to be employed there. The diverse patient population included Caucasians, Latinos, and African Americans, many of whom had never been treated by an African American doctor.

To maintain a credible private medical practice, Joseph also needed to obtain hospital admitting privileges outside of the University of Texas Health Center. At the time, several Austin hospitals had not accorded admitting privileges to Black doctors. Carefully navigating the path toward gaining privileges, Joseph sought professional recommendations from several Howard medical school professors, provided copies of his Yale and Howard transcripts, and gently leaned on the Yale University old boy network. His strategy secured admitting privileges at several hospitals.

During the earlier part of their time in Austin, Joseph and Arthuree again met with racial discrimination when they decided to live in an integrated neighborhood. Their initial attempts to locate suitable housing kept circling them back to the Black community. Upon discovering that an African American family wanted to purchase one of his lots in the exclusive Northwest Hills district, the property owner refused to sell to them. The Quanders quietly retained a builder who gave the appearance that he was going to live there himself. Once the house was built, the land and house were transferred through straw transactions to the Quander family. Ironically, a few years later, Joseph and Arthuree were invited to join a local real estate conglomerate that formed as a limited partnership to purchase much of the remaining acreage that was within the same section of Northwest Hills.

Joseph is a charter member of the Austin Chapter of Sigma Pi Phi (the Boule), a fraternity founded in 1904 in Philadelphia that consists of professional African American men of significant and sustained achievement. He was also inducted into the Omega Psi Phi Fraternity while enrolled at Howard University College of Medicine.

Now in his senior years, Joseph has witnessed many changes in the attitudes of Whites toward Blacks. He hopes his aspirations and successes contributed to that change and that others will see that his personal life and professional career have ably demonstrated that African Americans have always been and continue to be integral participants in what it means to be an American.

Joseph Aloysius Quander (1941–2019)

Joseph Aloysius Quander, who joined the DC Fire and Emergency Management Service in 1964, rose through the ranks while earning a BS degree in fire science from the University of the District of Columbia. Joseph's leadership characteristics led to appointments as director of the Fire Training Academy; fire marshal for the District of Columbia; and assistant fire chief in charge of the operations bureau, which consisted of the Firefighting Training and Communication Divisions. Mayor Marion Barry appointed him to the Police and Firefighters Retirement Board, where he ruled on requests for disability retirements filed by members of the Metropolitan Police Department, Uniformed Fire Fighters, the United States Park Police, and the United States Secret Service Uniform Division. Joseph was also appointed to the Building Code Advisory Committee, which revised and developed fire safety and construction codes for the city. He retired in 1999 at the rank of assistant fire chief, having given thirty-five years to protect and serve the residents of the District of Columbia.

Beyond his professional career as a firefighter, Joseph was an active church member, a fourth degree honorary life member of the Knights of Columbus, Washington, DC, and past president of the Board of Directors, Knights of Columbus, Bryne Council #3877 Home, Inc.

Sister Beatrice J. Jeffries (1946–2009)

Sister Beatrice Julia Jeffries, affectionately known as "Sister Bea," was born in Washington, DC, the tenth of the eleven children of Everett L. and Catherine Ann Gordon and granddaughter of Mary Ellen Quander Gordon. She professed her initial religious vows in 1967 after completing her novitiate with the Sisters of the Blessed Sacrament, an order founded by St. Katherine Drexel. Sister Bea made her final profession of vows to become a nun in 1972.

Sister Bea received a BA degree in education from Xavier University, New Orleans, and a master's degree in guidance and counseling from Trinity College, Washington, DC. She taught in parochial schools in rural Louisiana, Pennsylvania, New York City, Florida, Chicago, and Indiana. In every assignment, she brought joy and cheer to everyone while becoming deeply involved with the local community. In addition to her teaching duties, Sister Bea mentored Black history study clubs, coached girls' basketball teams, and served on parish councils and numerous parish school and church committees.

Well read, Sister Bea represented the face and status of Catholic women, serving as both vice president and the public face of her religious order. Both in word and action, she preached founder Katharine Drexel's message of love and justice for all peoples of color. She recruited women to join the congregation then taught and mentored sisters in training. She also authored a new African American vocation discernment prayer card that was widely disseminated. Pearlette Springer, a former student, in remembering Sister Bea, said, "In my youth, girls were not altar servers. So when she introduced liturgical dancing, it gave us girls a chance to be close to the altar. Without saying it, she made a statement that Black women and women in general were welcome in the church."

A deeply significant honor was given to Sister Bea when she was selected to deliver a scriptural reading during the canonization mass for St. Katharine in Rome on October 1, 2000. Among her many awards, Sister Bea received the Harriet Tubman award from the National Black Sisters Conference in recognition of her outstanding commitment to education and liberation of African American people. Often called "a Moses to her people," Sister Bea was sought after by religious congregations and dioceses to consult or facilitate on issues, including culture, power struggles, and community. She was noted for being able to say strong things in a nonconfrontational manner, thus winning the hearts of many and showing how to find common ground as she sought to keep dialogue open.

Paul Alonzo Quander Jr. (1954–2016)

Paul Alonzo Quander Jr. was born in Washington, DC, the elder son of Paul Alonzo Jr. and Roberta Jones Quander. His life was distinguished by success, achievement, and hard work. He graduated with honors twice: first from Virginia State University and again from Howard University School of Law. Paul was awarded a

Reginald Heber Smith Community Law Fellowship and elected to work for the Neighborhood Legal Services Program in Washington, DC, where his first clients were mostly indigents. Two years later, Paul accepted a position with the Corporation Counsel (now the Office of the Attorney General), where he distinguished himself not only as a hard worker but also talented beyond his young years as an attorney. He initially represented the city in diverse civil and criminal matters, but his skills directed him toward prosecuting criminal offenders.

Paul received the Corporation Counsel Award for Sustained Superior Performance in 1986 and 1987 and, in 1987, was named chief of the Correctional Litigation Section, where he served as general counsel to the DC Department of Corrections. In 1989, Mayor Marion Barry appointed Paul as deputy director of the department. In that capacity, he was responsible for twelve thousand prisoners in eight separate institutions. In 1994, Paul joined the U.S. Department of Justice (DOJ), United States Attorney's Office as an assistant U.S. attorney, and over the next seven years served in various capacities in the criminal section (prosecuting homicides, narcotics crimes, and organized crime), supervising appeals, and working with grand juries. Paul received DOJ Special Achievement Awards in 1997, 1998, and 1999 and was selected as the DOJ's Senior Litigation Counsel in 2000. He also received the DOJ Director's Award in 2005.

In 2001, President George W. Bush nominated Paul to serve as the first director of the Court Services and Offender Supervision Agency (CSOSA). During his six-year appointment (2002–2008), Paul made CSOSA a national model for offender supervision. As CSOSA director, he oversaw the supervision of 15,000 adults on probation, parole, and supervised release in the District of Columbia, managed a budget of $140 million, and supervised 900 employees while maintaining strict offender accountability, increasing community partnerships and implementing an award-winning performance management system. When asked how he measured success for CSOSA, Paul said a success occurred "every time an offender completes his term and goes on to pay taxes and attend his kids' PTA meetings."

In 2010, Paul became the deputy mayor for Public Safety and Justice in Washington, DC. As deputy mayor, Paul supervised and coordinated nine public safety agencies, including police, fire, and emergency medical services; corrections; homeland security; emergency management; unified communications; and forensic sciences and medical examiner. Energized by the enormity of the challenge and responsibility, Paul rose to the occasion to ensure the day-to-day safety and well-being of DC residents, employees, and visitors. He often commented that successfully fulfilling the myriad duties and responsibilities required of the deputy mayor was truly the pinnacle of his legal career.

Those who knew Paul will always remember his sharp intellect, quiet confidence, and vision, all which were enhanced by his leadership skills, personal integrity, and fairness in dealing with others. He painted a path to follow and left this place far better than he found it.

Michael Richard Quander Jr. (1989–)

Michael Richard Quander Jr. has distinguished himself as a television journalist, host, and public speaker. As part of his bachelor's degree in telecommunications from Morgan State University (Baltimore, Maryland), Michael completed internships at WEAA 88.9, the university's radio station, and Baltimore's WMAR-TV, where he accepted his first post collegiate job as an assignment editor and associate producer. Two years later, Michael was hired for his first on-air position at WREG-TV (Memphis, Tennessee), where he exposed city bus drivers breaking the law, investigated cronyism at city hall, and appeared on national news programs for coverage of a missing child and race relations in Mississippi.

In 2017, Michael relocated to the District of Columbia as a reporter at WUSA-TV, a local CBS affiliate, where he completed a short documentary on his family's history. *I Am Quander* aired in 2017 and, a year later, earned Michael his first Emmy Award for a special report about the Quander family history and African American genealogy. In 2019, Michael created and began hosting "For the Culture," a weekly WUSA segment that focuses of DC culture, history, and social issues unique to the Black community. Michael volunteers as an emcee and speaker at nonprofit organizations, schools, and charitable events. He has dedicated his life and career to be a voice for the voiceless, to inspire the next generation, and to make a positive impact in his communities.

Military Service and Leadership

Richard Ignatius Quander, second from
left, career military musician, c1899

Most of the men in this section are career military men. Several of the men listed above, including Peter Mercer Quander, Lewis Lear Quander, and Milton Ford Quander, also served our nation.

John Pierson Quander Sr. (1845–1925)

John Pierson Quander Sr. was born in Fairfax County, Virginia, the son of Lewis and Susannah Russell Pierson Quander. In 1863, on his eighteenth birthday, he enlisted in the U.S. Army as a private at Mason's Island, Virginia, and was assigned to Captain Hiram P. Thompson's Company "G," part of the First Regiment, U.S. Colored

Infantry. He was promoted to drill corporal in 1864 and, that year, fought in numerous battles or skirmishes, including Fort Fisher in North Carolina and Wilson's Landing, Petersburg, and Deep Bottom in Virginia. Quander also served as aide-de-camp in the Union army and carried the Union flag into battle. After the war, John married Hannah Bruce Ford (1850–1941), a granddaughter of Quander family ancestor West Ford. Most of John and Hannah's eight children, both daughters and sons, achieved educational and professional success as teachers. John Pierson Quander Sr. was buried at Arlington National Cemetery with full military honors on May 25, 1925.

Corporal John Pierson Quander, Sr. (1843-1925) in his Civil War uniform, 1915, Grand Army of the Republic reunion, colored department

Donald Victor Quander (1917–2002)

Donald Victor Quander was born and educated in New York City. His parents were Charles C. and Elizabeth Welch Quander. Beginning in his youth, Donald taught himself airplane mechanics by reading manuals, and later, he worked on airplanes and taught engine and radio mechanics to civilian students who wanted to learn to fly. He joined the U.S. Army Air Corps in 1941 and, after World War II, reenlisted in the newly created U.S. Air Force. In the Army Air Corps, Donald was assigned as an aircraft maintenance mechanic and electronics instrumentation specialist for the all-Negro 99th Pursuit Fighter Squadron, based in Tuskegee, Alabama. He also served with the 332nd Fighter Group. Although he was not an official U.S. Air Force fighter pilot, he flew frequently and could take off, land, and navigate. Later in World War II, when it became impractical to limit black mechanics to maintaining planes for Black pilots, Donald was reassigned to the recently integrated 79th Fighter Group, which was a mostly White pilot group. In spite of his loyal service, in Alabama, Donald endured many adverse racial experiences, including having the military police holding guns on the Black troops in the streets of Montgomery. As a New Yorker outspoken on civil rights matters, his attitude and refusing to move to the back of the bus in Tuskegee resulted in a severe beating.

Donald saw service in Morocco, Sicily, and Italy and spent several years in Japan. He was a lead composite character in *Red Tails*, the 2012 feature movie about the Tuskegee Airmen. After the war, he kept current as aviation technology changed. In the late 1940s, Donald was assigned to the staff that maintained the U.S. presidential aircraft, including Air Force One. He was a member of Euclid Lodge No. 70, Prince Hall Mason's New York Jurisdiction; St. Augustine's Episcopal Church in Newport News, Virginia; and the East Coast Chapter-Tuskegee Airman Inc. until his death. After a thirty-year military career, Donald V. Quander retired as a U.S. Air Force Chief Master Sergeant.

Charles J. Quander, Jr. second from right, U.S. Army Air Corps, with fellow Tuskegee Airmen

Leo Austin Brooks Jr. (1957–)

Leo Austin Brooks Jr. is the son of Naomi Lewis Brooks, a great-granddaughter of Charles Henry Quander of Spring Bank, Alexandria, Virginia, and Leo Austin Brooks Sr. Leo Jr. received his BS in mechanical engineering in 1979 from the U.S. Military Academy (West Point) and, in 1990, earned his MA in public administration from the University of Oklahoma. He began his 27-year military career in 1979 with the 101st Airborne Division, serving in developmental positions from platoon leader to infantry company commander. He was the first African American to command a Ranger company in the history of the modern Ranger Regiment. In Korea, he served on the joint staff of the Combined Forces Command. Upon completion of Brigade Command in 2001, Leo Jr. was selected for brigadier general and assigned as the deputy commanding general for operations of the 1st Armored Division in Europe. Among his more than fifteen career assignments, perhaps the most prestigious was his 2002 selection for the command of the U.S. Corps of Cadets at West Point as its 68th Commandant, the number two position at the academy.

Leo Jr.'s final position was as vice director of the army staff in the Pentagon, charged primarily with coordinating the army's efforts in support of the global war on terrorism. He has received numerous awards and decorations, including the Distinguished Service Medal (the third-highest army decoration); the Freedom Team Salute Award for outstanding service to the nation; the Black Engineer of the Year Military Leadership Stars and Stripes Award; and the Black Engineer of the Year Career Achievement in Industry Award. After retiring from the army in 2006, Brooks joined the Boeing Company's Washington DC office, first as its Army Systems vice president, and later as vice president of Enterprise Subsidiary Integration. He is among the top 60 executives in the 150,000-person company.

Vincent Keith Brooks (1958–)

Vincent Keith Brooks, Leo Jr.'s brother, entered the U.S. Military Academy (West Point) in 1976. Three years later, he was the first African American to be appointed as the cadet brigade commander, the top-ranked cadet leadership position, in charge of leading the more than four thousand cadets of all classes. Graduating in 1980 as a second lieutenant, Vincent served through all officer ranks. His overseas assignments included Germany during the Cold War; three separate commands in South Korea, the last of which was a joint U.S.-Korea command in which he was over the combined army, navy, marine corps, and air force forces in Korea; Kosovo (2001); and six years of service in the Middle East including Kuwait, Qatar, Iraq, and Afghanistan. In 2003, he was the U.S. Central Command's Deputy Director of Operations during the war in Iraq, a position that made him highly visible in the media. His deft handling of the media and his outstanding performance as the U.S. government's military spokesman earned him international recognition and respect. Millions of people around the world observed his daily televised press conferences.

Vincent earned the rank of brigadier general in 2002, the first graduate of West Point's class of 1980 to become a general, and in 2013, he was the eighth African American to become a four-star general. Over the course of his extensive career, Vincent received numerous accolades, medals, and badges. He concluded his forty-two-year military service in 2019.

The Generals Brooks—Record of Outstanding Achievement

The Generals Brooks—brothers Leo Jr. and Vincent and their father, Leo Austin Brooks Sr.—accomplished a national milestone as the only African American family in the history of our nation to have a father and two sons become generals in any military service. Leo Brooks Sr. (1932–) was educated in segregated public schools and earned a bachelor's degree in instrumental music education from Virginia State College, where he was president of both his Alpha Phi

Alpha fraternity chapter and the Student Government Association. Upon graduation, he was commissioned as a second lieutenant in the U.S. Army. He earned an MS in financial management from George Washington University and a doctor of laws from the New England School of Law in Boston. After thirty years of service, Leo Sr. attained the rank of major general but left the service early to become managing director of Philadelphia (1984–1985). In retirement, he has served on many boards, commissions, and councils, including the Board of Directors of USAA and the American Bar Association's Council of Legal Education and Accreditation of Law Schools.

The three Brooks generals were recognized for their lifetime achievement by the Urban League of Northern Virginia in 2019.

Four Quander family generals seen with Rohulamin
Quander; left to right—Gen. Leo Brooks, Sr.;
Gen. Vincent K. Brooks; Rohulamin Quander;
Gen. Mark Quander; and Gen. Leo Brooks, Jr.

Mark Christopher Quander (1973–)

Over the course of Mark Christopher Quander's life, his faith, determination, and dedication have come to define him. During his formative years, the family moved more than seven times as a result of his father's military reassignments. In West Germany, Mark played soccer, which often took the Quander family to East Berlin for sports matches. Witnessing the stark realities of communism was the beginning of Mark's journey of preserving the freedoms we all enjoy. He was also influenced by the biography of Henry O. Flipper, born a slave and the first African American to graduate from West Point, where he endured a four-year silence from his fellow cadets. During his senior year in high school, Mark observed U.S. service men and women being deployed to the Middle East for Desert Storm and Desert Shield. Their patriotism and enthusiasm spurred Mark to apply for the U.S. Military Academy at West Point, from which he graduated in 1995 with a BS in civil engineering and as a second lieutenant in the Corps of Engineers. Mark later enrolled in the U.S. Army Ranger School at Fort Benning, Georgia, followed by an initial assignment to the 82nd Airborne Division. He deployed to Afghanistan in 2002, where he participated in the first major conventional battle and served in several subsequent operations.

Mark's sustained military achievements led to his appointment as the 98th Commandant of the U.S. Army Engineer School at Fort Leonard Wood, Missouri, where he is in charge of the training of all engineer soldiers for the U.S. Army. Operating with a multibillion-dollar budget, he oversees and directs transatlantic construction programs and projects to ensure our tactical forces have the most up-to-date means of accessing fields of combat on very short notice. His many military awards include the Legion of Merit and the Bronze Star Medal. In February 2020, Mark earned the rank of brigadier general.

2018, Quanders gather at Maryland National
Capital Park and Planning Prince George's County
reception during Black History Month. The
theme, *African Americans in Times of War*, featured
World War I veterans Pvt. John E. Quander, Sr.,
and Corp. Peter M. Quander, Sr. and others

ABOUT THE AUTHOR

Rohulamin Quander, Author

Rohulamin Quander, a native Washingtonian, is a retired senior administrative law judge for the District of Columbia and holds a BA degree (1966) and a JD degree (1969) from Howard University. He is a member of the Quander Family, whose distinguished history traces to the 1670s in the Maryland and Virginia colonies. The Quander legacy includes George Washington's Mount Vernon Plantation's enslaved ancestors Sukey Bay, Nancy Carter Quander, and West Ford. Judge Quander periodically serves as an advisor to Mount Vernon, most recently for the exhibit Lives Bound Together,

Slavery at George Washington's Mount Vernon, and still maintains close ties.

In 1985, Judge Quander founded the Quander Historical and Educational Society, Inc. (QHES), a 501 (c)(3) foundation established to document, preserve, and share the historical legacy of the Quander Family, a product widely recognized as an inspirational and educational tool.

His continued years of service include addressing human and civil rights inequities and discrimination against the Dalit (untouchable) population of India, one of his maternal ancestral homelands. The author of three prior books, Judge Quander's current offering, *The Quanders—Since 1684: An Enduring African American Legacy*, relates the multi-century journey of one of America's oldest documented families who, despite racially imposed obstacles at each turn, through entrepreneurship and perseverance, triumphed to be included by a visit to the Oval Office and a recognition greeting by a U.S. president.

Judge Quander is a licensed District of Columbia tour guide. Married to Carmen Torruella-Quander, internationally acclaimed artist, they have three adult children and one grandchild. They reside in Washington, DC

NOTES

---◆◆◆◆◆---

Introduction

1. "To Be a Quander," a poem by Lewis Lear Quander, appears under his name in the Appendix.
2. Lewis Lear Quander wrote "Miracle of Faith" as a tribute to his many Quander, Lear, and other ancestors who served at George Washington's Mount Vernon Plantation. The occasion was the tenth anniversary observance, on September 18, 1993, of the 1983 dedication of the Slave Memorial placed at Mount Vernon by the Mount Vernon Ladies Association. The annual observance is held with the cooperative efforts of Black Women United for Action.
3. In addition to *The Quander Story*, I have published three other books: *Quander Quality: The True Story of a Black Diabetic* (2006), *Nellie Quander: Alpha Kappa Alpha Pearl* (2008), and *50+ Omega Inspired Years: Tracing an Omega Legacy to 1931* (2014).

Chapter 1

1. *Adams* also appears as *Addams* in the historical documents I consulted. I use the more traditional spelling of *Adams*.
2. Adams's service in the colonial government is recorded in Edward C. Paperfuse, et al., *A Biographical Dictionary of the Maryland Legislature 1635–1789*, Vol. 426, p. 98 (Archives of Maryland Online, http://aomol.msa.maryland.gov/html/index.html).
3. *Wills*, Charles County, Province of Maryland, Vol. 4, pp. 204–205, July 1686. Although the name "Quander" appears on a list of Melungeon Family surnames in the 1670s in Virginia, Adams's will is the first known official Quander family-related document.
4. It is not known where or when Henry and Margrett married or if they were ceremonially married. A subsequent court decision refers to Henry as having been born in 1675, which would mean he was approximately nine years old at the time Adams's will was written in 1684. Margrett and Henry were both young at the time of their manumission and probably did not marry until several years later.

[5] Henry's cattle mark is recorded in *Court and Land Records*, Charles County, Maryland, R1: 271, 1691.

[6] The freehold lease is recorded in *Deeds*, Charles County, Province of Maryland, Q1: 83–4, 1695. A map of the tract is available in Louise J. Hienton, "Map of Tract," Prince George's County, Maryland Hall of Records, Annapolis.

[7] The High Court's ruling against Henry's argument that Margrett was a free woman appears in *Land Records*, Charles County, A2: 80, 1702.

[8] The handwritten script of the early eighteenth-century document I consulted is difficult to read, and her surname might be *Ryney*. I elected to use the *Rannes* spelling as more probable.

[9] The lengthy court case between Margrett Quando and Thomas Wheeler is recorded in *Court and Land Records*, Charles County, 12:188, 201, 311; K2: 234–5, 1718–1722. Margrett's court-ordered award is noted in the same *Court and Land Records*, K2: 234–5, 1722.

[10] Margrett's petition and the court's favorable decision appear in *Judicial Records*, Prince George's County, pp. 312–313, June Court 1724. Subsequent rulings against her petition to be relieved of the tax levy are found in Prince George's County *Judicial Records*, p. 615, November Court, 1727; and p. 398, August 1733.

Chapter 2

[1] *Loving vs. Virginia*, 388 U.S. 1 (1967).

[2] The case against Victoria Quando is recorded in *Court and Land Records* (Deeds), Charles County, B:2: 186, 1705–06.

[3] The length of time between Victoria Quando being charged for bastardy and Mary Quando being cited for the same offense suggests that Victoria was possibly Mary's mother and not her older sister, thus rendering Mary a granddaughter of Henry and Margrett. For ease of narration, I've assumed Mary was their daughter.

[4] The March 1724 case against Mary Quando appears in *Lord Proprietary vs. Maria Quandoe*, Prince George's County *Judicial Records*, p. 420, 1723–26. "Lord Proprietary" referred to George I, Absolute Lord Proprietary, king of England. See also Prince George's County *Judicial Records*, p. 379, November Court 1724 with reference to the same offense.

[5] Mary Quando's second appearance before the court in June 1725 for having given birth to a bastard child is recorded in Prince George's County *Judicial Records*, p. 457, 1723–26.

[6] Mary Quando's final documented appearance before the court for her third illegitimate child is recorded in Prince George's County *Judicial Records*, p. 624, November Court 1727.

Chapter 3

1 *List of Taxables, 1733* (Lower Piscataway Hundred), Thomas Stonestreet, Calendar 270, Vol. II, p. 118.
2 *John Maddox, Assignee, Richard Cross vs. Henry Quando*, June 26, 1731 (Prince George's County *Judicial Records*, Book 8, Liber R, pp. 142–143).
3 The summons for John Maddox to return to a court hearing in June 1732 is recorded in Prince George's County *Judicial Records*, Book 8, Liber R, p. 631, June 1732.
4 *Henry Quando vs. Alexander Frazer*, August 25, 1732 (Prince George's County *Judicial Records*, pp. 66–67, 1732–33).
5 Henry II's case against Margorot and Samuel Clements for unpaid goods is recorded in Charles County *Judicial Records*, pp. 220–221 (June 9, 1741), 1741–43. His second suit against Clements on August 11, 1741 (*Henry Quando v. Samuel Clements*), for lack of payment for building a small house, appears in the same volume (pp. 249–250).
6 Henry II's estate is described in Prince George's County *Inventories*, Vol. 29, pp. 139–140, 1744.

Chapter 4

1 The performance bond for the estate of Margaret Godfrey Quando is recorded in Prince George's County *Bonds*, Box 19, Folder 37, 1776.
2 Various documents show *Suky* and *Sukey*. I have elected to use the latter.
3 A lineal descendant is the child, grandchild, great-grandchild, and so forth of a particular person.
4 Osmond Quander's holdings are noted in Luther Porter Jackson, *Labor and Property Holdings in Virginia, 1830–1860*, Appendix II, pp. 247–248.
5 Information concerning the 1793 Virginia General Assembly legislation was extracted from Donald Sweig, *Registration of Free Negroes for Fairfax County* (1977), an edited version of the many registrations that were recorded in the eighteenth and nineteenth centuries in the county. Similar registers existed for Alexandria County (now Arlington), the District of Columbia, and Maryland.
6 William, West Ford's older son, and William's wife, Henrietta Bruce, were the grandparents of eight Quander descendants through the marriage (c. 1870) of their daughter, Hannah Bruce Ford (1850–1941) to John Pierson Quander (1845–1925). Nellie May Quander (1880–1961), First Supreme Basileus of the Alpha Kappa Alpha Sorority, Inc., would become the best known Ford descendant. Major George William Ford, Nellie's cousin, was the first and, at the time, the only African American superintendent of the National Cemeteries, serving in that capacity from 1878 until 1930. He was also a member of the Niagara Movement, the spiritual pioneer that led to the creation of the NAACP in 1909. Other descendants of West Ford include many public school educators; a county commissioner in North Carolina; a university dean; several federal civil

servants and civic leaders; musicians and a poet actress; a newspaper reporter; prominent ministers in the Baptist, Methodist, Episcopal, and Congregational churches; athletes; and several who distinguished themselves in the medical, dental, and scientific professions.

[7] Sweig (p. 4) discusses the 1850s petitions from free Blacks to remain in Virginia.

[8] Much of the information provided about Charles Quander is based on the personal recollections of Gladys Quander Tancil or family stories she heard through the years. Therefore certain aspects, such as the exact date of an event, are not included as they would need further research to be verified or determined.

Chapter 5

[1] *Quando v. Clagett*, Case No. 11,492; 4 *Cranch Reports*, C.C. 17; 20 Fed. Cases, p. 105; Circuit Court, Dis. of Columbia, May 14, 1830. *Quando v. Clagett* is also available in William Cranch, chief judge of the Court, *Reports*, Vol. IV (Little, Brown and Company, Boston, 1852).

[2] *Marbury v. Madison*, 5 U.S. 137; 1 Cranch 137 (1803). Marbury was the plaintiff in this historical constitutional case, one of the earliest landmark cases heard by the U.S. Supreme Court that formally established the high court's right of judicial review.

[3] Brice Clagett advised me that the Thomas Clagett mentioned in Margaret Clagett's will was almost certainly the Thomas Clagett IV who resided at Weston, a plantation house just outside of Upper Marlboro, and Margaret's first cousin twice removed.

[4] Rhoda Glasgow's certified manumission appears in Prince George's County *Certificates of Freedom*, 1820–52, p. 98, CR #27,250.

[5] Harry Quando's petition appears in the National Archives Record Group 21, District Court for the District of Columbia, *Records of the U.S. Circuit Court*, Entry 1, Docket Book, Item 331, May Term 1830.

[6] Register of Historic Sites for Prince George's County, Survey P. G. 79-63, TM 93, Parcel 10, 1988.

[7] M-NCPPC report, Section 8, Significance, p. 3.

[8] *African-American Heritage Survey*, p. 90.

[9] Recollections of the house and yard are from interviews I conducted on April 1–2, 1996, with Francis, James, Paul, and Richard Quander. Sisters Henrietta Quander Walls and Christine Quander Simmons also contributed their recollections of meetings held under the walnut tree.

Chapter 6

[1] The initial charges against Felix and his wife and son appear in Fairfax County *Court Minute Book*, p. 278, 1867–69. The same volume contains *Common-*

wealth vs. Julia Quander (p. 285) and *Commonwealth vs. Felix Quander* (p. 286). "Joseph" appears among the Carter family given names at Mount Vernon during the slavery period.

2 The felony offense charges against Felix and Joseph appear in Fairfax County *Court Minute Book*, p. 318, 1867–69.

3 Joseph Quander's request to be released from jail and the court's response are recorded in Fairfax County *Court Minute Book*, p. 28, 1869–71.

4 Felix and Julia's confrontations with Landstreet are recorded in *Commonwealth vs. Quander*, Fairfax County *Court Records*, Term Papers, Box 31, November–December 1874.

5 The story of the posse's attack on the Quander family appeared in the March 24, 1879, editions of both the *Washington Republican* and the *Alexandria Gazette* (p. 3). All subsequent references to *Gazette* should be understood to refer to the *Alexandria Gazette*.

6 "Last of the Quander Case," *Alexandria Gazette*, May 24, 1879, p. 3.

7 In his lengthy letter to the editor (*Evening Star*, August 4, 1879) concerning the harness theft, Felix does not mention his son who received a gunshot wound to the head during the February 16, 1879 incident. Although previously referred to as a probably fatal injury, perhaps the injury was less serious.

8 *Alexandria Gazette*, August 4, 1879, p. 2.

Chapter 7

1 James Borchert, *Alley Life in Washington: Family, Community, Religion, and Folklife in the City, 1850–1970* (University of Illinois Press, Chicago, 1980).

2 The various sources I researched used the words *street*, *place*, and *alley* in referring to the Quander location. Because some of the more expansive recent studies use "place," I follow that designation.

3 The description of the location of Quander Place in Lot 23 is found in District of Columbia Office of Historic Preservation, *Determination of Eligibility Documentation: Quander Alley Archaeological Site, Washington, DC, Navy Yard Annex*. Report by Leo A. Daly, Soil Systems, Inc. (Alexandria, Virginia, May 26, 1982). All subsequent references are to the *Eligibility Report*.

4 Information about the August 1814 Battle of Washington is from Taylor Peck, *Round-Shot to Rockets: A History of the Washington Navy Yard and U.S. Naval Gun Factory* (U.S. Naval Institute, Annapolis, Maryland, 1949).

5 *Eligibility Report*, p. 8. Building 213 was constructed in 1944 to store naval guns and ammunition. After the war it became a top secret site and housed the National Photographic Interpretation Center (*The History of NPIC*, Lindsay Tilton Mitchell, February 17, 2016).

6 *Eligibility Report* contributed data about the 1900 U.S. Census (p. 8) and city housing density (p. 3).

[7]   "Pottery and Pig's Feet: Space, Ethnicity, and Neighborhood in Washington, DC, 1880–1940," *Journal of Historical Archeology*, Vol. 24, No. 1, 1990, pp. 34–57.

[8]   "Pottery and Pig's Feet," p. 35.

[9]   *Eligibility Report*, pp. 8–9.

[10] Charles Frederick Weller, *Neglected Neighbors* (John C. Winston Company, Philadelphia, 1909).

[11] Whether the "Harry" who lived at 109 Quander Place is the same person as "Negro Harry Quando" in the 1830 case *Quander v. Clagett* is doubtful, although there might be some connection between the two men.

[12] I conducted in-depth telephone interviews with both sisters on September 19, 1993, on life in Quander Place.

Chapter 8

[1]   Prohibition (1920–33) outlawed the production, transport, and sale of alcoholic beverages throughout the United States.

Chapter 10

[1]   *After the Revolution: Everyday Life in America, 1780-1800*, November 18, 1985–March 3, 2002. https://www.si.edu/exhibitions/after-revolution-everyday-life-america-1780-1800-event-exhib-3429

Chapter 11

[1]   Today's MVLA property comprises approximately five hundred acres of the original eight thousand acres of the Mount Vernon Plantation. https://www.mountvernon.org/about/

[2]   The mission statement on the MVLA website is as follows: "The mission of the Mount Vernon Ladies' Association is to preserve, restore, and manage the estate of George Washington to the highest standards and to educate visitors and people throughout the world about the life and legacies of George Washington, so that his example of character and leadership will continue to inform and inspire future generations." https://www.mountvernon.org/preservation/mount-vernon-ladies-association/

[3]   Mount Vernon archivist Rebecca Baird located the 1928 MVLA *Minutes* (which generally list neither a month nor an exact date) pertaining to the slave cemetery marker. The references from this document are as follows: "Mrs. Maxey," p. 46; "the graves will disappear," Tomb Committee report, p. 75; and "the marker should be of stone," p. 75.

[4]   The George Ford mentioned in the MVLA *Minutes* is the apparent son of Major George W. Ford (1847–1939), a Buffalo soldier and the first and only super-

intendent of a national cemetery (1878–1931). Major Ford was a grandson of West Ford. However, George II's statement is somewhat suspect, as allegedly there were no burials at the site in the twentieth century.

5 Extract from a 1994 statement by Dr. Lillian D. Anthony reprinted in the Black Women United for Action (BWUFA) annual Slave Memorial program, October 1, 2016. The remainder of this account is based on my interview of Dr. Anthony in the late 1990s.

6 Dorothy Gilliam, "Remembrance," *Washington Post*, February 6, 1982.

7 The genesis of the Slave Memorial is recounted in *The History of the Slave Memorial at Mount Vernon* (undated), published by BWUFA and MVLA.

8 Governor Robb's remarks are from *Fairfax Chronicles*, Nov. 1983–Jan. 1984, Vol. VII, No. 4, pp. 1–2.

9 A collateral descendant is a relative descended from a brother or sister of an ancestor.

10 The description of the Slave Life Tour relies on Gladys's recollections and Rhonda Henderson, "Mount Vernon's Other Legacy," *City Paper*, Washington, DC, August 25, 1995.

11 *Lives Bound Together: Slavery at George Washington's Mount Vernon*. https://www.mountvernon.org/plan-your-visit/calendar/exhibitions/lives-bound-together-slavery-at-george-washington-s-mount-vernon/

Chapter 12

1 Several Quanders, including myself, have confirmed our Ghanaian ancestry through DNA testing.

2 These are the exact words the Ghanaian man said to me during my highly emotional moment in the Room of No Return. I wrote them in my travel journal immediately upon exiting the dungeon area.

Epilogue

1 Fath Ruffins was project director for the exhibit, *After the Revolution: Everyday Life in America*.

2 Both the Elmina and Cape Coast castles, located in Ghana's Cape Coast region, have a Quander-Amaquandoh legacy. Although my personal experience occurred at the Elmina Castle, the photographic exhibit was set up at the Cape Coast castle, which has a professional exhibit area. The two slave castle sites are approximately eight miles apart.

Appendix

1 The family surname is spelled three ways in the Sacred Heart church record: *Quando*, *Quander*, and *Quand*.

2   According to their descendants, many Quander family men were Knights, including James Augustine Quander (former president who also served as president of the Beneficial), Richard Eugene Quander, Paul A. Quander, Francis A. Quander, James A. Simmons (president, 1955–75), James L. Simmons, William D. Simmons, and Lawrence Henry.

3   Information about Mount Calvary was retrieved from Mount Calvary Baptist Church Anniversary Booklets, 1976–2016.

4   The story of the KKK in Brooklyn was recounted by Howard W. Quander, Charles's son, in an interview with Bernice Johnson Reagon of the Smithsonian Institution's Center of Family Life.